PACIFIC PROFILES

VOLUME 10
Allied Fighters: P-47D Thunderbolt series
Southwest Pacific 1943–1945

MICHAEL JOHN CLARINGBOULD

Avonmore Books

Pacific Profiles Volume 10

Allied Fighters: P-47D Thunderbolt series Southwest Pacific 1943–1945

Michael John Claringbould

ISBN: 978-0-6457004-0-4

First published 2023 by Avonmore Books

Avonmore Books
PO Box 217
Kent Town
South Australia 5071
Australia

Phone: (61 8) 8431 9780
avonmorebooks.com.au

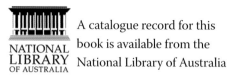

A catalogue record for this book is available from the National Library of Australia

Cover design & layout by Diane Bricknell

Front Cover: The wide range of Thunderbolt colour schemes which appeared in New Guinea is evident here. From top to bottom are the 9th FS (Profile 1), the 341st FS (Profile 68), 39th FS (Profile 16), 310th FS (Profile 45) and the 69th FS (Profile 40).

Back Cover: A 342nd FS Thunderbolt tangles with a 59th Sentai Ki-43-II Hayabusa over Wewak in early 1944.

Contents

Contents 3

About the Author...5

Introduction 6

Glossary and Abbreviations 11

Chapter 1 – Markings and Technical Notes 13

Chapter 2 – 9th Fighter Squadron "Flying Knights".................. 21

Chapter 3 – 36th Fighter Squadron "Flying Fiends".................. 27

Chapter 4 – 39th Fighter Squadron 33

Chapter 5 – 40th Fighter Squadron "'Fightin' Red Devils".......... 39

Chapter 6 – 41st Fighter Squadron "Flying Buzzsaws"................ 43

Chapter 7 – 69th Fighter Squadron "The Fightin' 69th".............. 49

Chapter 8 – 310th Fighter Squadron 55

Chapter 9 – 311th Fighter Squadron... 63

Chapter 10 – 340th Fighter Squadron "The Minute Men"........... 71

Chapter 11 – 341st Fighter Squadron "The Black Jacks"............ 79

Chapter 12 – 342nd Fighter Squadron "The Scourgers" 89

Chapter 13 – Fifth Fighter Command Headquarters.................. 99

Chapter 14 – Combat Replacement Training Center 103

Sources & Acknowledgments... 107

Index of Names.. 108

The author, third from left, in Port Moresby in 2003 celebrating a field trip to the B-17E "Swamp Ghost" wreck. The others are (left to right) helicopter pilot Manu, Pacific historian and explorer John Douglas and Justin Taylan (the proprietor of website www.pacificwrecks.com).

About the Author

Michael Claringbould – Author & Illustrator

Michael spent his formative years in Papua New Guinea in the 1960s, during which he became fascinated by the many WWII aircraft wrecks which lay around the country and also throughout the Solomon Islands. Michael subsequently served widely overseas as an Australian diplomat throughout Southeast Asia and the Pacific, including in Fiji (1995-1998) and Papua New Guinea (2003-2005). Michael has authored and illustrated numerous books on Pacific War aviation. His history of the Tainan Naval Air Group in New Guinea, *Eagles of the Southern Sky*, received worldwide acclaim as the first English-language history of a Japanese fighter unit, and was subsequently translated into Japanese. An executive member of Pacific Air War History Associates, Michael holds a pilot license and PG4 paraglider rating. He continues to develop his skills as a digital aviation artist and illustrator.

Other Books by the Author

Black Sunday (2000)

Eagles of the Southern Sky (2012, with Luca Ruffato)

Nemoto's Travels –The illustrated saga of an IJN floatplane pilot (2021)

Operation I-Go – Yamamoto's Last Offensive – New Guinea & Solomons April 1943 (2020)

Pacific Adversaries Series

Vol One – Japanese Army Air Force vs Allies New Guinea 1942-1944 (2019)

Vol Two – Imperial Japanese Navy vs Allies New Guinea & Solomons 1942-1944 (2020)

Vol Three – Imperial Japanese Navy vs Allies New Guinea & the Solomons 1942-1944 (2020)

Vol Four – Imperial Japanese Navy vs Allies – The Solomons 1943-1944 (2021)

Pacific Profiles Series

Vol One Japanese Army Fighters New Guinea & the Solomons 1942-1944 (2020)

Vol Two Japanese Army Bomber & Other Units, New Guinea & Solomons 1942-44 (2020)

Vol Three Allied Medium Bombers, A-20 Series, South West Pacific 1942-44 (2020)

Vol Four Allied Fighters: Vought F4U Corsair Series Solomons Theatre 1943-1944 (2021)

Vol Five Zero Fighters (land-based) New Guinea & Solomons 1942-1944 (2021)

Vol Six Allied Fighters: Bell Airacobra South & Southwest Pacific 1942-1944 (2022)

Vol Seven Allied Transports: Douglas C-47 South & Southwest Pacific 1942-1945 (2022)

Vol Eight – IJN Floatplanes in the South Pacific 1942-45 (2022)

Vol Nine Allied Fighters: P-38 series South & Southwest Pacific 1942-1944 (2022)

South Pacific Air War Series (with Peter Ingman)

Volume 1: The Fall of Rabaul December 1941–March 1942 (2017)

Volume 2: The Struggle for Moresby March–April 1942 (2018)

Volume 3: Coral Sea & Aftermath May–June 1942 (2019)

Volume 4: Buna & Milne Bay June-September 1942 (2020)

Volume 5: Crisis in Papua September – December 1942 (2022)

Solomons Air War Series (with Peter Ingman)

Volume 1: Guadalcanal August – September 1942 (2022)

Osprey Publications

P-39 / P-400 Airacobra versus A6M2/3 Zero-sen New Guinea 1942 (2018)

F4U Corsair versus A6M2/3/4 Zero-sen, Solomons and Rabaul 1943-44 (2022)

P-47D Thunderbolt versus Ki-43 Hayabusa New Guinea 1943/44 (2020)

A6M2/3 Zero-sen – New Guinea 1942 – Dogfight Series (to be released 2023)

Introduction

This volume focuses only on the P-47 Thunderbolt fighter which operated in the New Guinea theatre of the South West Pacific Area (SWPA).[1] The Thunderbolt lacked the range to take the fight to Rabaul, and neither did it serve with the Thirteenth Air Force in the South Pacific. The *modus operandi* of all SWPA Thunderbolt units changed markedly after they left New Guinea as the war moved northwards towards Japan, after which the type's primary purpose switched to ground attack.

More Republic P-47 Thunderbolts were produced than any other US fighter in World War Two; more than 15,000 were built, of which around six hundred served in the SWPA, all "razorbacks". It was the biggest and heaviest single-engine fighter produced in the war, with a fully configured all-up-weight approaching eight tons and eight 0.50-inch calibre Browning machine guns housed in its wings. In New Guinea at least, its weight proved a real handicap as its take-off requirements and all-up-weight excluded it from operating at several forward airfields.

The first batch of Thunderbolts arrived in Australia on 27 June 1943 at Brisbane's wharves, prior to being trucked to nearby RAAF Amberley where they were assembled. The batch comprised 85 P-47D-2s, however they lacked external fuel tanks as USAAF Materiel Command had sidelined the 200-gallon tank designed for the type as it caused excessive tail buffeting. The first solution was to customise the flat 100-gallon tanks as used with the Airacobra and P-40E, however Patterson Field in the US could not build them in sufficient numbers. Instead, the 27th Air Deport at Seven-Mile 'drome, Port Moresby, modified the 100-gallon tanks themselves, and were soon fitting seven a day to the first 348th FG Thunderbolts.

By 1 August 1943 the same air depot had designed and built a 200-gallon tank later manufactured in Brisbane by the Ford Motor Company which came to be known colloquially as the "Brisbane Tank". Release and mounting mechanisms were soon fabricated, and it was convenient that spare booster pumps provided for the 100-gallon tanks were up to the task of fuel transfer. Units started replacing the 200-gallon "Brisbane Tank" with 160-gallon wing-mounted fuel drop-tanks around late January 1944. The 160-gallon tanks were widely available in the theatre, and two could be carried which increased the extra fuel capacity to 320 gallons. Later larger elongated oval-shaped 200-gallon drop tanks were modified so that they too could be fitted to the Thunderbolt. The shape and size of the fuel tanks on the Thunderbolt throughout 1943 were unique to the SWPA theatre.

On 16 August 1943, 32 P-47Ds initiated the first Thunderbolt mission of the Pacific war, escorting C-47s to a new grass airfield behind Lae at Marilinen. However, the Thunderbolt's arrival heralded a planning problem for USAAF operations officers. Until it showed up, a blunt round nose on a single-engine aircraft had always meant a Japanese fighter. Old habits die hard,

---

1   The SWPA included the Netherlands East Indies and the Philippines, where many Allied air force squadrons saw service in the last year of the war. However, in this volume the term "SWPA" refers only to the New Guinea theatre.

particularly under duress, and on several occasions Lightning pilots opened fire on Thunderbolts thinking they were Japanese. In late 1944 this resulted in one confirmed fatality when 348th FG pilot Lieutenant Adrian McCleldon was shot down by a flight of three Lightnings. This meant, where possible, patrols comprised of the two types of fighters were spaced and/or staggered. Not surprisingly feelings between Thunderbolt and Lightning pilots ran high whenever there were incidents, which unfolded more often than sanitised history presents. Thunderbolt pilots routinely referred to the Lightning as the "eggbeater".

Throughout its SWPA service, numerous and varied minor modifications were made to the Thunderbolt by both service and host squadrons. These were not always universal but included the fin antenna mount raised to increase radio reception, and the gun sight elevated by two inches to facilitate sighting. Some units cut a door into the rear fuselage side to more readily access the intercooler, and in March 1944 several units modified the electrical releases to jettison wing tanks. Constant niggly modifications attended these fuel pylons, as often depending on the tank size, it was discovered that jettisoned tanks could damage ailerons and flaps. Tyre blowouts were common, causing numerous accidents, and one modification was to electrically spin the main wheels before touchdown, thus reducing the chance of blowout. All these field modifications were researched and conducted, in particular, by the 61st, 66th and 482nd Service Squadrons at Nadzab.

However, the Thunderbolt suffered the disadvantage in the SWPA of being viewed at worst as a poor cousin to the P-38, and at best an interim solution until more Lightnings arrived. Hence Thunderbolt operations commenced with more benign assignments such as escorting transports to give pilots combat experience. These branched into escorting bombers to combat areas such as New Guinea's northern coast. The most aggressive phase was when the type was deployed as a short-range fighter, with Fifth Air Force fighter command deploying elite groups of Thunderbolts to the Wewak area where, on their own terms, they could engage unwary enemy aircraft.

Architect of the type's SWPA *modus operandi* as a fighter was Colonel Neel Kearby, initially the commanding officer of the 348th Fighter Group before being transferred to Fifth Fighter Command. Kearby tailored Thunderbolt doctrine to suit its strengths, emphasising that pilots should never break strict rules of engagement laid down for good reason. Above all they were never to engage the enemy in a low energy state, where superior Japanese manoeuvrability could be lethal.

Numerous works to date referencing the history of the Thunderbolt in the SWPA fail to underline its disappointing SWPA record which at times verged on the disastrous. All narratives of the highest-achieving Thunderbolt combat unit, the 348th FG, portray the popular image of success: a superior type carving its way through inferior opposition, earning disproportionately favourable combat results. This curious and bogus narrative derives from accepting Allied claims at face value instead of cross-checking with relevant Japanese records, and not consulting the USAAF field maintenance logs. Armed with this information, the type's true combat record in New Guinea of misfortune and lacklustre results comes into sharp focus.

The 348th FG Group lost 35 Thunderbolts to non-combat accidents before incurring its first combat loss on 22 October 1943. By the time it left New Guinea this despairing loss figure had increased to 51, including weather-related losses. About half of these incidents incurred fatalities or serious injuries, against a total of only nine airframes lost directly to combat. Thus, we can see that the SWPA Thunderbolt pilot was five times more likely to lose his life to weather or a landing or take-off accident than Japanese fighters.

The 58th FG, which was the last Thunderbolt unit to arrive in New Guinea, incurred even more breath-taking numbers of non-combat losses. In only their first month of operations the group lost scores of P-47s to accidents, with the losses of sufficient magnitude that Fifth Fighter Command delayed the unit's entry to combat. Then, on 2 February 1944 eight of the group's Thunderbolts drew a benign escort assignment of C-47 transports for their first combat mission. Thunderbolt *Louisville Lady* aborted the mission for no apparent cause, followed by four more which returned early to Finschhafen, three with engine trouble and the fourth to escort the others.

The 39th FS, a veteran SWPA fighter unit, in particular felt bitter when they had to trade their Lightnings for Thunderbolts in November 1943. Republic later sent out representatives to "sell" the Thunderbolt to pilots in early 1944 however these gatherings at Nadzab verged on the confrontational when pilots with hardcore combat experience challenged Republic's test-condition performance data. Later in July 1944, civilian legend aviator Charles Lindberg made presentations on how to extend the Thunderbolt's range, citing his experience in doing the same with the F4U in the Solomons, an airframe which shared the same R-2800 radial engine. Whilst his technical suggestions did extend the Thunderbolt's range, they also incurred extended low altitude cruises over water. Such flying was far from ideal where enemy fighters might be encountered. Later, it was found that the increased manifold pressure and low RPM sustained long-term damage to the engine. In the end, the innovation came to little; due the nature of Pacific geography, and despite high hopes to the contrary, Lindberg's initiatives did not change the type's *modus operandi*.

New Guinea pilots immediately discovered that New Guinea's humid and hot air offered thin air density, and thus poor performance which was particularly dangerous when "low and slow". These characteristics made flying the Thunderbolt a risky proposition during landing. In fact, the first loss in theatre was due to such factors on 15 August 1943, when Lieutenant John Schrik lost control on approach in rotor turbulence, spinning the fighter into the ground and killing him. The fighter's high wing loading meant long runways were required for take-off, particularly so when loaded with either extra fuel tanks or bombs.

Neither did the type prove superior in combat in the SWPA despite every Allied history telling you otherwise. Even in the last Thunderbolt battle of 1943, the Japanese were contemptuous of the fighter's lack of manoeuvrability. On 26 December 1943 eight 248th *Sentai* Ki-43-II *Hayabusa* encountered sixteen 36th FS P-47Ds and shot down two without loss. Of this encounter Japanese commander Major Muraoka Shinichi later wrote:

When we met Thunderbolts they immediately surrounded and separated us from protecting the Donryu [bombers]. *They attacked from above, outnumbering us three or four to one, however we lost no fighters. In conclusion we did not lose, and one Hayabusa which failed to drop one of its fuel tanks survived. I am of the firm opinion that the Thunderbolt can be shot down if we take advantage of its mistakes. Four enemy Thunderbolts only amount to one or two of our planes . . .*

On 5 March 1944 Colonel Neel Kearby departed Nadzab with two Fifth Fighter Command comrades, Captains Sam Blair and Bill Dunham. They approached Wewak airspace at 22,000 feet and below spotted four 208th *Sentai* Ki-48 Lily light bombers in Dagua airfield's circuit. The flight dived and shot down three in short order, however the intrusion alerted five 77th *Sentai* Ki-43-II fighters. These launched from Dagua in two separate flights: a trio led by commanding officer Major Matsumoto Kunio and a pair led by Warrant Officer Mitoma Koichi. Kearby then violated his own dictum by never turning at low altitude, a manoeuvre he likely made to ascertain the fate of the victims. As he was turning, a Ki-43-II *Hayabusa* fighter made a beam attack. Kearby banked towards Dunham's protective gunfire, however it appears Kearby himself was hit in this process. Warrant Officer Mitoma Koichi and Sergeant Aoyagi Hiroshi, one of Matsumoto's wingmen, each claimed a Thunderbolt. Aoyagi had barely arrived in theatre with only about 200 hours of flying, and his attack drove Kearby into foothills behind Dagua airfield.

In concluding the type's lacklustre combat record, the Thunderbolt's last New Guinea combat engagement of 11 April 1944 was also disastrous. With Wewak's airfields no longer operational, sixteen Ki-43-II *Hayabusa* and eight Ki-61 *Hien* from Hollandia led by 33rd *Sentai* commander Captain Namai Kiyoshi patrolled Wewak's airspace. Nonetheless his modest formation doggedly attacked about one hundred incoming USAAF aircraft including sixteen 58th FG Thunderbolts. Five P-38s downed two Ki-61 *Hien*, the only Japanese losses despite generous US claims otherwise. Recalling Fifth Air Force commanders' reluctance to permit the 58th FG to enter combat, the unit's Thunderbolts had only been permitted to fly on this mission as no enemy contact was expected. The first 58th FG Thunderbolt shot down was *Fascinatin' Phil*, which crashed into hills near Boram airfield. It was followed by two more victims, Major Thomas Bullington in *Cowtown Cyclone* and Lieutenant William Graham. Namai claimed one of these, later reporting that the battle had been "one-sided" in Japanese favour.

Many older Thunderbolts stayed behind in New Guinea right until the end, used for training purposes with the Combat Replacement Training Center (CRTC) based at Nadzab. The CRTC was a mammoth composite outfit, supported by the 360th and 8th Service Groups. The latter outfit sustained the only loss of a female in a fighter in New Guinea. This occurred on 5 May 1945 when Lieutenant Harold Wurtz took Miss Harriet Gowan, an American Red Cross nurse, for a joy flight in an 8th Service Group P-47D. The fighter failed to return and in fact crashed at high speed, with the wreck not discovered until 1996.

The reality is the Thunderbolt made little impact on the New Guinea air war; its limited range sidelined it from both the Rabaul and Hollandia campaigns, and its first series of limited engagements achieved nowhere near the favourable kill ratios still held aloft today. During the Thunderbolt's heyday, most Japanese activity had ceased along New Guinea's northern shore. Post-war data shows that Thunderbolt pilots in New Guinea, alongside their Japanese counterparts, overclaimed their aerial victories on an average of about four to one.

The opportunity for air combat all but evaporated once the Thunderbolt left New Guinea. With Japanese aerial opposition all but wiped out by March 1944, in the later Netherlands East Indies and Philippine campaigns the Thunderbolt was used primarily as a ground-attack aircraft as increasing numbers of "bubbletops" entered service.

Michael John Claringbould
Canberra, Australia
November 2022

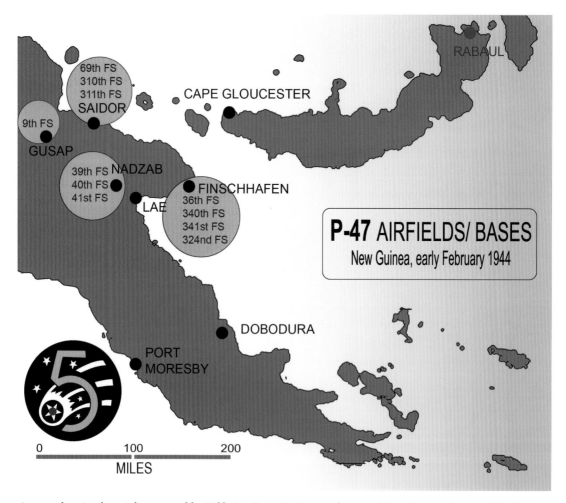

A map showing key airbases used by Fifth Air Force P-47 squadrons in New Guinea during 1943-1944. Lacking the range to reach Rabaul, Thunderbolts mainly saw service along New Guinea's northern coastline where Japanese bases were located to the west of this map. P-47s also served with the Combat Replacement Training Center at Nadzab in an operational training role as late as mid-1945.

Glossary and Abbreviations

Note: Japanese terms are in italics. All Japanese names are presented in the traditional way of writing Japanese, with the surname presented first.

BG	Bombardment Group
CRTC	Combat Replacement Training Center
FG	Fighter Group
FS	Fighter Squadron
Hayabusa	Peregrine Falcon (JAAF name for Ki-43 "Oscar" fighter)
Hien	Flying Swallow (JAAF name for Ki-61 "Tony" fighter)
Hiko Sentai	A JAAF Flying Regiment, often abbreviated to *sentai*.
Hinomaru	The red disc on the Japanese flag representing the sun and also used as a roundel on Japanese aircraft.
IJN	Imperial Japanese Navy
JAAF	Japanese Army Air Force
MIA	Missing in Action
MSN	Manufacturer's Serial Number
RAAF	Royal Australian Air Force
RPM	Revolutions per minute
Sentai	Abbreviation of *hiko sentai* defining a JAAF flying regiment.
SWPA	South West Pacific Area
US	United States
USAAF	United States Army Air Force

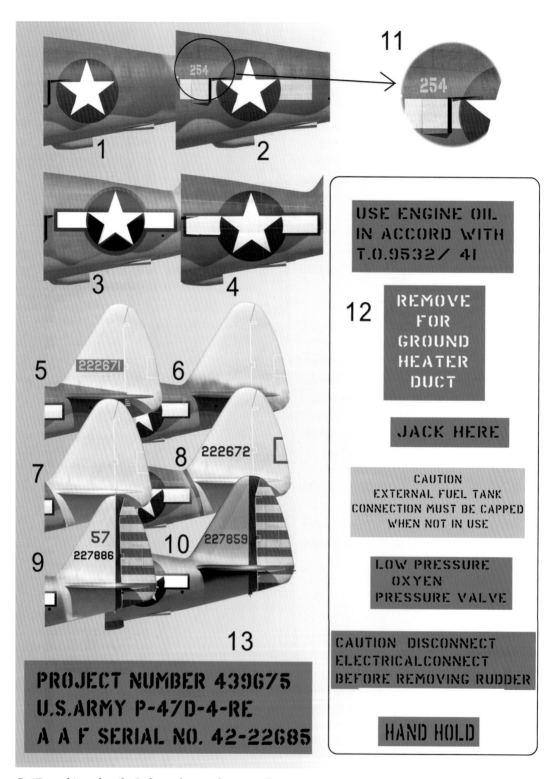

P-47 markings details. Refer to the text for an explanation.

CHAPTER 1
Markings and Technical Notes

It is regrettable that Thunderbolt markings in the SWPA continue to be misrepresented with an ongoing litany of errors which has been caused by, *inter alia*: manufacturer's numbers confused for squadron numbers or as the last part of a serial number, changes of squadron numbers during unit exchanges, and hybrid markings misinterpreted as unit ones. Another source of confusion stems from a failure to recognise cowl swaps. Particularly decorative (and often expensive) nose-art was retained when newer models arrived often by keeping previous cowls and fitting them to the incoming airframe. This happened a lot, with three examples appearing in this volume alone: Profiles 39 and 40 *Sleepy Time Gal*, Profiles 69 and 70 *Daring Dottie III* and Profiles 83 and 84 *Sylvia*. Remarkably, some early D model cowls were still flying on P-47N "bubbletops" in late 1945!

Another source of confusion is interpreting yellows as whites from monochromatic films, such that 69th FS Thunderbolts are mistaken for those from the 310th FS and *vice versa*. The 58th FG is a particular casualty for misidentification for another reason: several photos of the P-47Cs in which they trained in the US have been labelled as taken in the SWPA. These Thunderbolts, many of which had names and nose-art, did not serve in the SWPA and in fact no P-47C reached the theatre.

The 1st Composite Fighter Unit served with the Combat Replacement Training Center at Nadzab, and four of these examples are illustrated for the first time. This remains truly a forgotten unit. As a final caution, Thunderbolt markings in the SWPA changed markedly after they moved to the Netherlands East Indies and then northwards to the Philippines and beyond. That era forms no part of this work. The transition of theatres involved, for a start, a complete reworking of tail designs.

National Insignia

The ubiquitous US insignia of white star in blue circle which had been extant since 1919 first appeared with a small red circle in its centre. On 12 May 1942 the US Army issued technical orders to remove this circle, along with pre-war red, white and blue rudder stripes which still attended a variety of airframes in 1942. This is ironic given that SWPA Thunderbolt units reverted to adopting this tailplane marking in mid-1944 once they started acquiring natural metal finish airframes. The first batch of these were P-47D-20s which arrived in the theatre in early May 1944, followed by larger batches of natural metal finish P-47D-23s. The first natural metal finish P-47 to arrive in the SWPA was P-47D-20 serial 42-25410 delivered to Port Moresby by 340th FS pilot Captain Otto Carter, who later became deputy commander of the 460th FS in the Philippines.

National Insignia diagrams as illustrated on page 12:

1. This standard US insignia appeared on all P-47D-2 airframes and the first batches of P-47D-3s leaving US factories from May 1942 until May 1943. Accordingly, the first batch of Thunderbolts taken up by the 348th FG carried this marking on an Olive Drab airframe. Note that the single circular marking was applied more forward on the fuselage than the later "star and bar" insignia, a giveaway to identifying earlier model Thunderbolts.

2. US Army tests proved that at a distance, especially in the air, it was easier to discern shapes than colours, so bars were added to the roundel with a red outline to accentuate the shape against an Olive Drab background. The relevant Army/Navy (AN) Markings Specification AN-1-9A was introduced on 28 June 1943, with the first red-bordered insignia applied in Republic's factory in July 1943. However, due to its obvious colour association with the *hinomaru*, the Fifth Air Force informed Washington two months later that they would be painting out the red border for security reasons. In the field, the single circular star had the white bars without blue piping added as illustrated here.

3. Later batches of P-47D-2s in the 42-22XXX range and then those within the P-47D-3, -4 and -11 series had the red-bordered star and bar applied in the factory. These were often painted over in insignia blue, grey or even black in the field.

4. Largely due to complaints from the Fifth Air Force, the red outline was replaced with a dark blue outline via the AN-I-9A specification promulgated on 14 August 1943. Technical Order 07-1-1 issued on 24 September 1943 ordered amendments to extant field markings, however these were not implemented by Thunderbolt units until October 1943. All batches of P-47D-11s and subsequent Olive Drab Thunderbolts left the factory with the revised dark blue outline star and bar.

Tailplane Markings

The Fifth Air Force started painting the tailplanes of all its fighters white, including wing leading edges, as early as July 1943. These markings were applied so that Allied fighters could be more easily identified in combat, and also by Allied ship and ground gunnery units. Whilst the official directive was promulgated in September 1943, there was a lag of several months before the convention became universal. The varying quality of water-based or acrylic white paints resulted in different weathering patterns. Overall, these white theatre markings were another example of a Fifth Air Force initiative being adopted by Washington after the fact. The practice of white-tailed fighters had become universal throughout the SWPA by January 1944 and the Thirteenth Air Force, to a limited extent, adopted the practice too.

Tailplane marking diagrams as illustrated on page 12:

5. Most units chose to mask the serial number before spraying or painting the fin. However, this was not always the case, and there were numerous examples where serials were painted over which made it difficult to identify individual fighters, a practice prominent in the 9th FS.

6. Note that the delineation of the border on the fin varied considerably. In this example we see a curved rubber mat was used to mask a low-pressure spray application.

7. In many instances a mask was taped to the airframe resulting in a clean line.

8. Rather than masking off the serial number, some units reapplied it after the tail was painted, either in yellow or black stenciling. Some units painted the trim tab border in red, not to be confused with overspray from poor masking, giving the appearance of a painted line in some black and white photos.

9. Many of the first natural metal finish Thunderbolts to arrive in the theatre, beginning with the P-47D-23 series, also had their tails painted white. The practice seemed a token one in some cases as later on the high visibility red, white and blue rudder scheme was applied over the tail.

10. By the time Thunderbolt units were leaving the SWPA, the practice of painting tailplanes white had been abandoned.

Notes on Airframe Stencils as per the diagram on page 12:

11. The Manufacturer's Serial Number (MSN), sometimes referred to as either the Manufacturer's Number (MN) or Constructor's Number (CN) was stenciled in yellow on Olive Drab airframes, often and erroneously illustrated in white. It was stenciled in black on natural metal finish airframes, and the stencil was applied on both sides of the fuselage in the same location. The stencil was often removed in the field by ground crews, so the number was not confused with squadron numbers or USAAF serial numbers, explaining why it fails to appear in many photos of the era. This is particularly true in the case of natural metal finish airframes where the MSN was easily removed with emery paper. No reference to MSNs appears in unit maintenance logs – aircraft were uniquely identified by (USAAF) serial number. The style of MSN stencil varied slightly with models and batch numbers and was not always applied horizontally. Another anomaly is that the MSN was not applied at the factory among some batches.

12. This series of self-explanatory airframe stencils appeared on various parts of the airframe. Some ground crews reapplied the stencils in white so they were easier to read. Other service units applied their own unique stencils which referred specifically to field modifications, particularly those pertaining to drop shackles.

13. This stencil appeared only on the forward port side of the fuselage underneath the cockpit and is Republic Aircraft's manufacturing stencil. The Thunderbolt was manufactured in three different factories across the US. Most output came from Farmingdale on Long Island, New York, (identified by an "RE" suffix in the serial block). The other sites were Evansville, Indiana, (with an "RA" suffix) and the Curtiss Aircraft Plant in Buffalo, New York, (although none from the Buffalo plant left the US mainland). Even though the USAAF issued guidelines on stencil formats and sizes, these in practice varied to a limited extent depending on the factory.

Notes on USAAF Serial Numbers as per the diagram on page 17:

There were also minor variations to the USAAF Serial Number within batch and production runs. There were variations to the style of stencil applied on the fin in the factory. These were sometimes modified in the field when stencils were reapplied over white tails or following repairs. Here are four examples of the variations.

14. This was the standard yellow stencil style as applied to the early models from P-47D-2s through to early batches of D-11s.

15. This cut stencil style commonly appears as a field stencil as applied by service squadrons from Port Moresby to Nadzab, usually applied in a matt finish.

16. This factory example was traced from the tail of 42-75921 which force-landed in Australia during a ferry run. Note that the stencil is thin and that the 7 has a unique and less-slanted style. The style is common to late batches of P-47D-11s.

17. This style is common to natural metal finish P-47D-23s and was applied in semi-gloss black.

Notes on Propellers as per the diagram on page 17:

Whilst there were four different propellers fitted to the P-47 series throughout production, three electric and one hydraulic, the Curtiss electric series was standard to the New Guinea theatre. The 12-foot two-inch Curtiss Electric thin blade was installed in the Evansville factory on all models through to the P-47D-21 (Evansville plant), however the 13-foot one-inch paddle-blade was installed on the P-47D-23 series onwards. The two types were interchangeable in the field.

18. The data stencil applied to the prop by Curtiss. The Max and Min data refers to the angle of attack of the propeller blade, specifically to the 12-foot two-inch series.

19. The Curtiss wartime manufacturer's logo pertaining specifically to their electric propeller series.

Two 348th FG ground crew sit on the wing of MSN 241 at Ward's 'drome, Port Moresby, in September 1943, linking it to P-47D-2 serial 42-8093. The tail had already been painted white before ferrying from Australia. Note the unpacking list taped to the fuselage just ahead of the MSN.

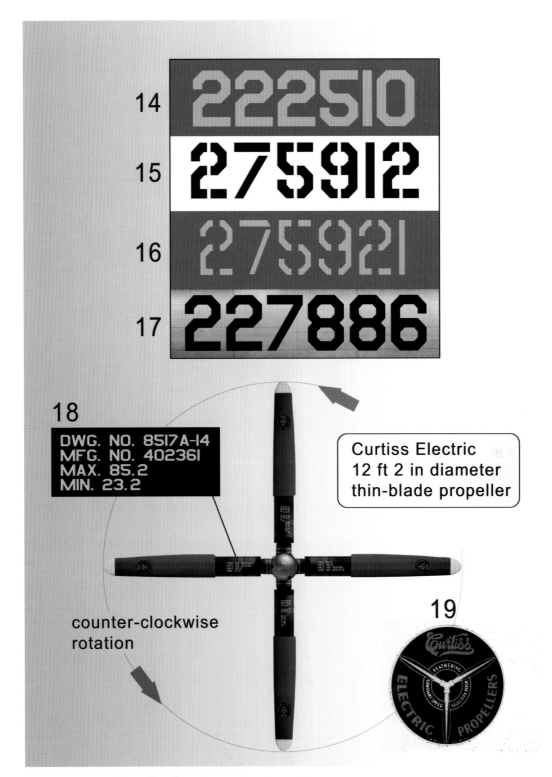

14 **222510**

15 **275912**

16 **275921**

17 **227886**

18

DWG. NO. 8517A-14
MFG. NO. 402361
MAX. 85.2
MIN. 23.2

Curtiss Electric
12 ft 2 in diameter
thin-blade propeller

counter-clockwise
rotation

19

Further P-47 markings details as discussed in the text.

P-47D-2 serial 42-8067, MSN 215, at Port Moresby just after arriving in the theatre in July 1943. Note the fighter lacks a squadron number. This Thunderbolt later joined the 342nd FS where it was named Bonnie.

End of the road for dozens of "razorback" Thunderbolts ready for scrapping at Nadzab in late 1945. A close examination reveals representation from nearly every Fifth Air Force Thunderbolt group.

Cosmoline inhibitor is washed off the airframe of a new P-47D-16 just assembled by the 27th Air Depot at Seven-Mile 'drome, Port Moresby, in early 1944. These boxed airframes were unloaded at Tatana Wharf, before being delivered by truck along Baruni Road for assembly.

A 1,000-pound bomb is loaded on a wing pylon. These release shackles underwent numerous modifications in the New Guinea theatre. This "bubbletop" Thunderbolt appears in the Philippines.

P-47D-11 serial 42-23109 is towed after assembly through Brisbane's streets just behind Eagle Farm airfield around July 1944. From here it will be delivered to the 35th FG at Nadzab. Note that the anti-glare panel extends all the way along the cowl, not always the case in later model natural metal finish "razorbacks".

Taken at Guam, well outside the New Guinea theatre, the natural metal finish on this "bubbletop" Thunderbolt nonetheless reveals the degree to which some crews polished the airframes. The polish reputedly added around five knots to the cruise speed.

Taken at Seven-Mile in late May 1944, this is one of the first natural metal finish Thunderbolts to arrive in the theatre, among a batch of 28 P-47D-20s. It was assembled at the Commonwealth Aircraft Factory in Melbourne and delivered via Horn Island equipped with two 160-gallon wing-mounted tanks for the journey. Note that it is already fitted with a swapped-over Olive Drab cowl, doubtless to keep the nose art on the other side, the identity of which we are not privy. Such swaps have confused the real identity of many original Thunderbolt airframes.

CHAPTER 2
9th Fighter Squadron "Flying Knights"

Having operated P-38 Lightnings for most of 1943, the 9th Fighter Squadron's subsequent association with the P-47 Thunderbolt was one of disappointment. When the first batch of sixteen Lightnings had been assigned to the squadron in Townsville in October 1942, they were allocated to an "outsider" contingent of ex-Java pilots newly assigned into the unit. These pilots then languished in Townsville pending a full complement of P-38s which did not arrive until January 1943. Thus, the squadron's eventual acquisition of P-38s was viewed as hard-won. It is easy to understand their resentment when they were taken away from them.

On 6 March 1943 the 9th FS moved their Lightnings to Dobodura, using them well throughout 1943 and becoming fond of the type. Disappointment peaked in October 1943, when it was announced that due to ongoing shortages of Lightnings, all of the squadron's P-38s would be transferred to the 475th FG and replaced by P-47D Thunderbolts. The squadron's pilots viewed the new type with disdain. They undertook conversion to the Thunderbolt in 35th and 348th FG P-47Ds until assigned their own Olive Drab Thunderbolts ranging from the P-47D-2 to -16 variants. They flew these to Gusap in early January 1944 from where they operated until April 1944. From Gusap the 9th FS transferred to Dutch New Guinea and then the Philippines, after re-equipping with Lightnings. The squadron was the only one of the 49th FG's three squadrons to operate the P-47.

Major Gerald Johnson, appointed 9th FS commander on 1 October 1943, oversaw the squadron's transition to the Thunderbolt. In late December 1943, when seconded to the 36th FS for training purposes, he flew Thunderbolt "H" too close to a nervous B-25 gunner who shot out his hydraulics. Johnson then had to belly-land at Nadzab, although the incident was logged as an operational accident with no reference to weapon discharge. Johnson returned to the US on 29 January 1944 for leave and command training and was replaced by Major Wallace Jordan. The squadron's Thunderbolts had meanwhile moved to Gusap in the Ramu Valley. During the Gusap phase the 9th FS flew mainly patrols and fighter sweeps along the northern New Guinea coast. Operations were constrained by the type's limited range, and fighter escorts to distant Hollandia were left to the Lightings. Furthermore, enemy fighter activity had all but disappeared in the Wewak area by the end of February 1944 so opportunities for combat engagement were limited.

The 9th FS lost no Thunderbolts to combat, however it sustained several non-combat losses at both Nadzab and Gusap. It is difficult to ascertain the exact number, however, as several of the Nadzab Thunderbolt losses were technically assigned to other units when they were lost.

Markings

The 9th Fighter Squadron's Thunderbolts were numbered 70 to 99, with all numbers within this range used at one stage. A challenge for historians is that most airframes had their serials painted over in white, meaning many 9th FS Thunderbolts continue to elude identification.

Several older Thunderbolts received from other units already had the serial masked off, leaving it exposed. Around mid-January 1944 Johnson authorised that the forward cowl of the squadron's Thunderbolts be painted white as a unit marking. The style of calligraphy when marking each fighter differed considerably, and although cowl numbering was ubiquitous, some tails were not numbered. Although many fighters were named, the squadron lacked an experienced artist, with much art being rudimentary.

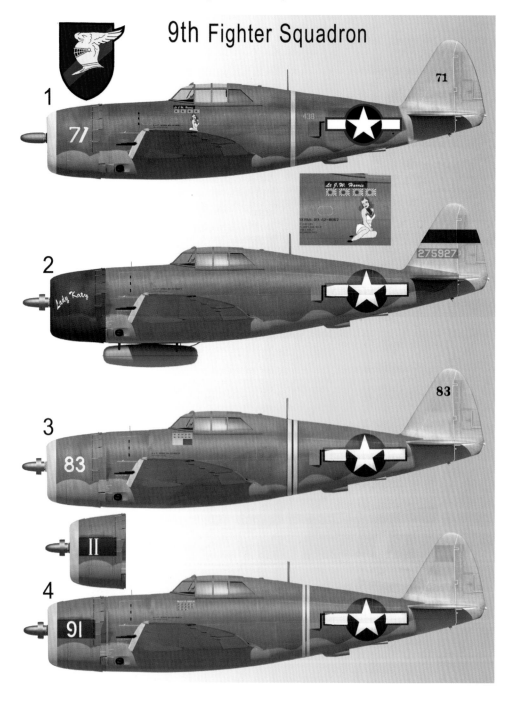

9th Fighter Squadron

Profile 1: P-47D-16 serial 42-22687, MSN 438, squadron number 71

This Thunderbolt was reassigned into the 9th FS from the 348th FG and allocated to Lieutenant James Harris at Gusap in January 1944. The Japanese flags represented Harris' four prior victories when flying a P-38 in 1943. The white vertical stripe had red piping denoting Harris' role as a flight leader. The star-and-bar insignia retained its red outline throughout the fighter's service. The crew chief painted the girl underneath the port cockpit, with red hair and a blue necktie. The aircraft carried no nickname and the number 71 was hand-painted on the cowl in reverse italic style, with the same number applied in unique calligraphy on the tail. The MSN 438 was stenciled in yellow on the rear fuselage.

With the 9th FS converting back to P-38 Lightnings in April 1944, this aircraft was transferred to the CRTC at Nadzab. On 29 April 1944 Lieutenant Marion Lutes departed Nadzab to conduct a weapons test over nearby Faita airfield. Lutes made no contact after take-off and remains MIA. The wreckage was identified in 1979, without Lutes, high in the Finisterre Mountains. It appears Lutes suffered an engine failure and tried to crash-land into trees. Nearby opened food cans indicate he survived the crash, before he likely died of exposure trying to reach safety. The Thunderbolt was salvaged in 2004, permitting detailed examination of its markings which were well preserved from its high-altitude resting place of 8,200 feet.

Profile 2: P-47D-16 serial 42-75927, *Lady Katy*

The matt black cowl resulted from over-painting the aircraft's previous unidentified 348th FG nose-art. The fin had a black band which covered one of the 348th FG squadron markings of red, yellow or blue. The fighter, one of the first assigned into the 9th FS inventory, is illustrated as it appeared during its first few weeks at Gusap, yet to be allocated a squadron number. In April 1944 it was reassigned to the 58th FG. The fighter is illustrated with a 200-gallon "Brisbane Tank".

Profile 3: P-47D-11 serial unknown, squadron number 83

This fighter was reassigned to 9th FS commander Major Gerald Johnson at Dobodura from the 348th FG in December 1943. Note the red piping on the twin command stripes which featured on several of the squadron's command and flight leader Thunderbolts. The feature is hard to see on black and white photos, resulting in flawed illustrations.

Profile 4: P-47D-16 serial unknown, squadron number II, then 91

When Johnson was appointed deputy commander of the 49th FG in early January 1944, he was allocated a new Thunderbolt. Its previous unknown squadron number was painted over and replaced by the Roman numerals "II" to represent his second-in-command status. Johnson's thirteenth kill was scored in this P-47D, a Ki-43 over Wewak on 18 January 1943. When Johnson returned home on leave on 29 January 1944, the score was painted over, the aircraft renumbered 91 and reassigned to his replacement Major Wallace Jordan.

9th Fighter Squadron

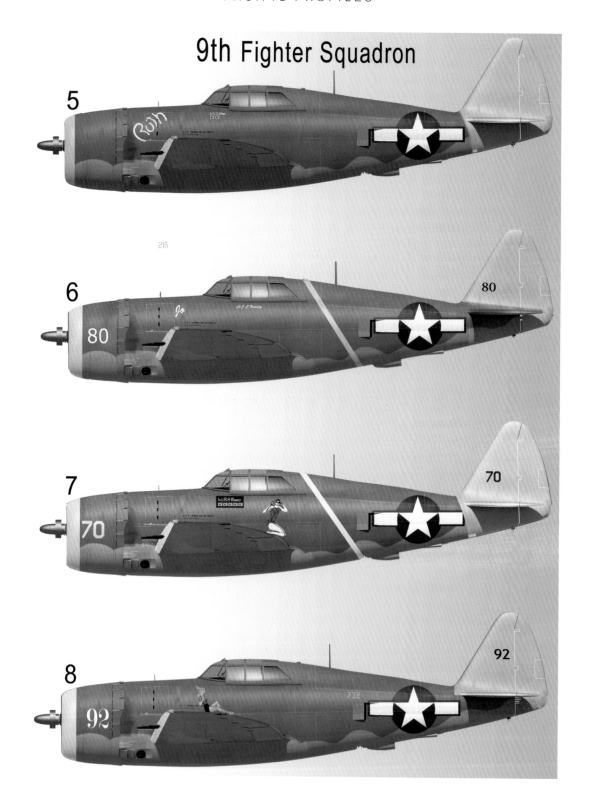

Profile 5: P-47D-16 serial unknown, *Ruth*

Illustrated as it first appeared at Gusap, awaiting a squadron number, this Thunderbolt was assigned to Lieutenant George Alber who named it after his fiancé and future wife, Ruth. Alber trained pre-war as a meteorological officer at Chanute Field in Illinois, joining the Army Air Corps in 1939 before earning his commission in March 1942. He flew Lightnings with the 9th FS from March 1943 to late January 1944, followed by 45 missions in the P-47D. Alber married Ruth in March 1944 and stayed on in the USAF as a meteorology officer. In 1954 he flew F-86 Sabres in Korea, and died on 4 Feb 2009 at age 90. The two flags represent victories Alber claimed when flying P-38s.

Profile 6: P-47D-16 serial unknown, squadron number 80, *Jo*

Assigned to Lieutenant James Haislip, this fighter had an oblique flight leader's command stripe.

Profile 7: P-47D-16 serial 42-75896, squadron number 70

Assigned to flight leader Lieutenant Ralph Wandrey, his crew chief painted the girl on the fuselage however the fighter was not named.

Profile 8: P-47D-11 serial 42-22981, MSN 732, squadron number 92

This unnamed Thunderbolt with a Vargas calendar girl was written off following a landing accident at Gusap on 9 February 1944 when flown by Lieutenant Wilbert Arthur.

A formation of 9th FS Thunderbolts fly over the coast just east of Finschhafen. Squadron number 77 is a P-47D-11.

Major Gerald Johnson stands on the wing of the subject of Profile 4 in January 1944 at Gusap. Note both ailerons are already painted white to assist with identification of his Thunderbolt in the air.

Lieutenant Howard Oglesby with his Bigasburd at Gusap around February 1944, an unidentified P-47D-16.

Lieutenant James Harris sits in his P-47D-16 serial 42-22687, the subject of Profile 1, at Gusap.

CHAPTER 3
36ᵗʰ Fighter Squadron "Flying Fiends"

The 36ᵗʰ FS conducted the first Airacobra combat of the Pacific War on 6 April 1942 over Port Moresby and operated the type in New Guinea until November 1943. After converting to the later P-39N and Q models in mid-1943, in late October 1943 the squadron commenced transition to P-47Ds, with eighteen on charge by early November at Wards 'drome, Port Moresby. It soon moved to Finschhafen, and then to Nadzab in early 1944. The 36ᵗʰ FS operated the Thunderbolt for only two more months before converting to P-38s in March 1944. During its time in New Guinea it lost two airframes to combat and two to other causes.

The squadron logo was a gargoyle-style beast with blooded tongue and bloodshot eyes wearing a leather helmet.

Markings

The 36ᵗʰ Fighter Squadron's Thunderbolt identification markings initially replicated the system previously applied to their Airacobras with each fighter assigned an alphabetical letter, painted on the engine cowl in white. This was in the form of a forward-leading italic attended by a white flying wing. Around January 1944 it dropped the wing motif and started replacing the letters with numbers. Serial numbers were masked off when the entire tailplane was painted white in accordance with the Fifth Air Force "friend and foe" requirements. The cowl doors were painted white, giving a vertical band behind the cowl. Spinners as a rule were also painted white.

P-47D-16 serial 42-75939 over Huon Gulf, showcasing the white spinner often applied by the 36ᵗʰ FS.

36th Fighter Squadron

9

10

11

12

Profile 9: P-47D-3 serial 42-22604, MSN 355, squadron letter G

This Thunderbolt is profiled as it appeared at Port Moresby in December 1943 when it was assigned to Lieutenant Gordon Giroux. The letter G was secured for his surname, and Giroux later painted two victory flags on the other side from two claims he made over Cape Gloucester on 26 December 1943. The fighter was reassigned to the 58th FG around March 1944.

Profile 10: P-47D serial 42-22630, MSN 283, squadron letter F

This Thunderbolt was assembled at the Commonwealth Aircraft Factory in Melbourne in November 1943.

Profile 11: P-47D-2 serial 42-8106, MSN 254, squadron letter E, *Collingswood, N.J. Legionaire*

This fighter was assigned to Lieutenant Edward Milner in late October from the 348th FG. Milner was from Atlanta, Georgia, however the fighter was named by a party unknown in honour of the town of Collingswood located near Philadelphia, New Jersey. The town has strong Quaker influence, and the word *Legionaire* refers to the founders of the movement which arose in England from the Legatine-Arians faction. On 26 December 1943, whilst covering US landings at Cape Gloucester on New Britain, a formation of 36th FS Thunderbolts was attacked by JAAF Ki-43-IIs. Lieutenant Arthur Heckerman was shot down in this fighter but ditched successfully half a mile north of Silimati Point and was rescued by a USN destroyer.

Profile 12: P-47D-3 serial 42-22608, MSN 359, squadron letter P

This fighter was assembled at the Commonwealth Aircraft factory near Melbourne in November 1943. It was assigned into the 36th FS in January 1944 after being flown to Nadzab via Brisbane, Townsville, Horn Island and Port Moresby. It was transferred to the 58th FG in March 1944.

P-47D-16 serial 42-75939 releases a wing-mounted fuel tank for the camera over the Markham Valley as part of a modifications trial. This Thunderbolt was later transferred to the 58th FG.

36th Fighter Squadron

Profile 13: P-47D serial unknown, squadron letter A, *Thunderjug*

This fighter was among the first batch assigned to the 36th FS at Wards 'drome from the 348th FG. It received the initial letter "A"; however, the letter was one of the few which was not italicised. It was transferred to the 58th FG at Saidor in March 1944.

Profile 14: P-47D-16 serial unknown, squadron number 17, *Ferocious Fagan*

This fighter was likely a new P-47D-16 delivered to the 36th FS at Nadzab around early February 1944. It was named by a Lieutenant Perkins (full name unknown).

A 36th FS Thunderbolt over Nadzab.

The proud ground crew of 36th FS P-47 "S" at Nadzab. The sign under the wing reads "Keep your dammed hands OFF THIS AIRPLANE".

Squadron number 19, a 39th FS Thunderbolt on final approach to Nadzab.

Lieutenant John Frost sits on the wing of squadron number 19 at Gusap. Note the decorated wheel hubs.

CHAPTER 4
39th Fighter Squadron

After commencing operations in New Guinea in 1942 with the Airacobra, the 39th FS flew its first combat in the P-38 Lightning in late November 1942, during which time Major Richard Ira Bong, the future Fifth Air Force leading ace, was assigned to the squadron at 14-Mile 'drome, Port Moresby. The 39th FS operated P-38s for just over a year before transitioning to the P-47D on 21 November 1943. Much to the bitterness of the unit's pilots, the squadron's entire P-38 inventory was reassigned to the 475th FG.

An initial batch of nine pilots was sent to Port Moresby for Thunderbolt transition training by squadron commander Major Harris Denton, while the rest remained at Nadzab. By February 1944, the 39th FS had 27 P-47Ds on charge. The squadron's pilots were reluctant to part with their Lightnings, more so since they had been the first unit to take the Lightning to combat in the SWPA. The 39th FS was assigned mostly hand-me-down early model Thunderbolts from the 348th FG until it received P-47D-23 natural metal finish Thunderbolts in June 1944. In July 1944 the famous aviator Charles Lindberg spent two weeks with the 35th FG at Nadzab teaching cruise control to the P-47 pilots, as he had previously done for P-38 pilots in other units. During its time in the SWPA the 39th FS lost ten Thunderbolts to non-combat causes, one to enemy strafing and two to aerial combat.

The 39th FS logo was a cobra in the clouds, deriving back to the unit's P-39 Airacobra days.

Markings

Allocated squadron numbers were applied in the 10 – 39 range, with the front of the cowl painted in a blue asymmetric design. White piping was applied to the blue shape on Olive Drab airframes and black on the natural metal finish ones. Many of the Thunderbolts were named and decorated, however there was no dedicated squadron artist, so the nose art was modest, mostly applied by their own ground crews or pilots.

P-47D-23 serial 42-27859, the subject of Profile 19, shortly after it left the New Guinea theatre.

39th Fighter Squadron

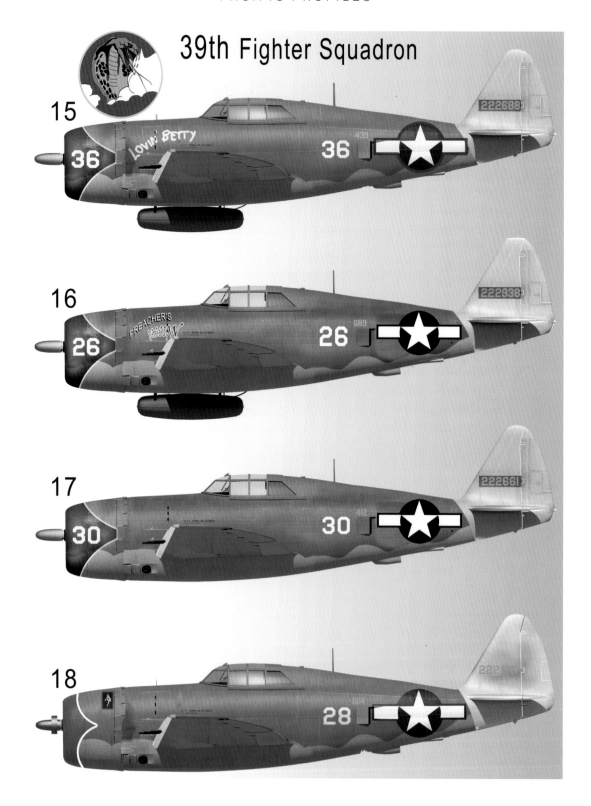

15

16

17

18

Profile 15: P-47D-3 serial 42-22688, MSN 439, squadron number 36, *Lovin' Betty*

This Thunderbolt was photographed at Gusap in early 1944 and is illustrated with a "Brisbane Tank". The fighter retained its red surround whilst at Gusap and later at Nadzab.

Profile 16: P-47D-11 serial 42-22938, MSN 689, squadron number 26, *Preacher's Passion*

Lieutenant William Rogers named this Thunderbolt which was destroyed on 19 April 1944 in an accident at Gusap when flown by Lieutenant Nick Fallier. It was replaced by *Preacher's Passion II*, and later a natural metal finish *Preacher's Passion III*. Rogers subsequently served as the 39th FS operations officer in late 1944. When he returned to the US, Rogers became a priest and later wrote his memoirs of flying the Thunderbolt in New Guinea in a fictional format titled *Outcast Red*.

Profile 17: P-47D-3 serial 42-22661, MSN 412, squadron number 30

This Thunderbolt was assigned to Lieutenant Robert Thorpe who departed Gusap on 27 May 1944 to strafe Japanese installations at But airfield near Wewak. Thorpe ditched the aircraft, likely due to damage from ground fire, and swam ashore to Kairiru Island. He was captured and taken to the IJN headquarters at the previous St John's Mission where three days later he was interrogated by IJN officer Lieutenant Commander Okuma Kaoru. The following afternoon at 1632 Thorpe was executed, with his body buried in a makeshift grave. A radio message outlining the execution to Truk was later intercepted, and Okuma was executed in 1949 for the crime. Attempts to locate Thorpe's grave post-war have been unsuccessful and at time of publication he remains MIA.

Profile 18: P-47D-11 serial 42-22913, MSN 664, squadron number 28

This fighter operated with the 39th FS at both Gusap and Nadzab throughout the first half of 1944 and was later scrapped at Nadzab. Note that the serial number was repainted over the white tail and that the squadron number was not applied to the forward cowl, which was decorated with a small Vargas calendar girl.

P-47D-3 serial 42-22688 Lovin' Betty, the subject of Profile 15, at Nadzab mid-1944.

39th Fighter Squadron

19

20

21

22

Profile 19: P-47D-23 serial 42-27859, MSN 1521, squadron number 23

The first natural metal finish Thunderbolts allocated to the 35th FG's three squadrons (the 39th, 40th and 41st FS) were received in June 1944. Deliveries did not always go smoothly – on 9 June 1944 Lieutenant Thomas Davis ran out of fuel when ferrying one from Townsville to Port Moresby. He ditched 50 miles southeast of Port Moresby however prevailing winds fortunately carried him to land. Here he was discovered by locals who helped return him to Port Moresby. Note that this natural metal finish Thunderbolt, one of the first assigned to the 39th FS, has no black piping on the blue cowl motif.

Profile 20: P-47D-23 serial 42-27609, MSN 1271, squadron number 33

Lieutenant Leroy Grosshuesch was assigned this natural metal finish fighter at Nadzab in June 1944. He had initially acquired considerable Thunderbolt experience when previously serving with the 439th FS at Tallahassee, Florida. It appears with seven kill markings, however, the fighter was left in New Guinea when Grosshuesch was promoted to squadron commander (see Profile 21). The fighter overturned during a take-off accident at Dobodura (Girua) airfield on 16 December 1944 and was abandoned. It was recovered post-war to Australia.

Profile 21: P-47D-23 serial 42-27861, MSN 1523, squadron number 10

At the young age of 24, Lieutenant Leroy Grosshuesch was promoted to captain and appointed 39th FS commander in November 1944. He chose squadron number 10 for his Thunderbolt, the first allocated number in the squadron. Note the two blue command stripes to denote his command position. Grosshuesch finished the war with 150 combat missions in both P-47s and later P-51s after moving to the Philippines. This fighter was destroyed during a mid-air collision over Clark Field in the Philippines on 19 May 1945 after it had been transferred to the 58th FG.

Profile 22: P-47D-23 serial 42-26394, MSN 1971, squadron number 18, *Little Country Gentleman*

This Thunderbolt was assigned to Lieutenant Jim Querns, an amateur artist fond of cartoons. He first painted Daisy Mae underneath the cockpit as it appears in the top cutout, the femme fatale from Al Capp's comic strip *L'il Abner*. This was later removed and replaced by two more cartoon characters (one starboard and one port) from the series *L'il Iodine*. The fighter then bore the stenciled name *Little Country Gentleman*.

Taken at Finschhafen, Lieutenant Leroy Grosshuesch sits on the wing of P-47D-23 serial 42-27609, the subject of Profile 20, his new natural metal finish squadron number 33.

A new 40th FS Thunderbolt on the flightline at Nadzab in June 1944.

An unidentified pilot poses with a natural metal finish Thunderbolt at Gusap in July 1944.

CHAPTER 5
40th Fighter Squadron "'Fightin' Red Devils"

The 40th FS arrived in Brisbane, Australia, on 25 February 1942 on the liner SS *Ancon*. It operated Airacobras throughout 1942 and by late 1943 had received late model P-39N and Q models. The squadron's Airacobras moved to Nadzab on 15 October 1943 where on 23 November 1943 the type performed an airshow for a United Service Organizations troupe led by Hollywood star Gary Cooper. At the time the unit's pilots were hopeful of transitioning to the P-38, however it was not to be.

The 40th FS instead converted to the P-47D in January 1944 whilst at Nadzab, before moving to Gusap from the end of February until June. The unit returned to Nadzab from mid-June until August 1944 after which it left New Guinea. The 40th FS pilots were not as bitter as their 39th FS contemporaries about receiving the Thunderbolt as they were "upgrading" from the Airacobra, and not "downgrading" from the P-38. The squadron's pilots considered the Thunderbolt a fast aircraft, but in terms of combat regarded it only as useful at high altitude, tempered by its lack of range. When the 40th FS transitioned again to P-51 Mustangs in the Philippines, the majority of its Thunderbolts were transferred to the 58th FG.

The 40th FS commander during the unit's Thunderbolt era from 12 February 1944 was Captain James Herbert. He was replaced on 5 May 1944 by Captain John Young. Whilst the squadron lost no Thunderbolts to combat, it lost eleven to accidents for reasons which include a mid-air collision, hitting a jeep on landing, take-off and landing accidents, and two engine failures. To underline the dangers of operating the type in low-energy state, on 11 March 1944 Lieutenant John Gerrity spun in from low altitude when pulling a tight turn during an aerial chase of an enemy fighter over the northern New Guinea coast.

Markings

The 40th FS allocated squadron numbers in the 40 to 69 range, with the front of the cowl painted in a red asymmetric design which varied on each airframe. White piping was usually applied to the motif on Olive Drab airframes and black on the natural metal finish ones. Relatively few of the squadron's Thunderbolts were named and decorated. With no dedicated squadron artist, any modest nose art was applied by squadron ground crews or pilots. Neither the 40th FS nor its sister unit the 41st FS painted squadron numbers on the cowls.

40th Fighter Squadron

23

24

25

26

Profile 23: P-47D-16 serial 42-75933, MSN 4284, squadron number 42, *Melanie*

This airframe entered service at Gusap in January 1944 and was among the first to add the 40th FS red lightning flash on the fin somewhere around May/June 1944. For unknown reasons the practice ceased with the arrival of the first natural metal finish Thunderbolts. Note the cut-in masking of the white tail application.

Profile 24: P-47D-11 serial 42-75290, MSN 3641, squadron number 56

This Thunderbolt was assembled at the Commonwealth Aircraft Corporation factory near Melbourne in January 1944 before delivery to Gusap shortly thereafter. It was lost to a take-off accident at Nadzab #3. Flown by Lieutenant Philip Thomas, it crashed about two miles southwest of the strip. Note the unusual extension of the red border line over the blue circle in the star-and-bar, applied by ground crew for decorative purposes.

Profile 25: P-47D-23 serial 42-27902, MSN 1564, squadron number 53

This natural metal finish Thunderbolt was assembled at the Commonwealth Aircraft Corporation factory near Melbourne in June 1944 before delivery to Gusap shortly thereafter. Although having natural metal finish, the tailplane was still painted white, and given a replica of the pre-war "Stars and Stripes" rudder marking. It went on the serve in the Philippines.

Profile 26: P-47D-23 serial 42-27886, MSN 1548, squadron number 57, *Miss Lorraine*

This natural metal finish Thunderbolt was assembled at the Commonwealth Aircraft Corporation factory near Melbourne in 1944. After initial use with the 342nd FS (see Profile 84) it was transferred to the 40th FS. It later served in the Philippines.

P-47D-23 serial 42-27886 Miss Lorraine, the subject of Profile 26, taxis at Morotai shortly after arriving there from the New Guinea theatre.

P-47D-23 serial 42-27902, the subject of Profile 25, in company with another 40th FS Thunderbolt at Nadzab in August 1944.

An unusual red nose application appears on a 40th FS P-47D at Eagle Farm, Brisbane.

CHAPTER 6
41ˢᵗ Fighter Squadron "Flying Buzzsaws"

The 41ˢᵗ FS moved its Airacobra operations to Tsili Tsili in August 1943 and then to Nadzab in December 1943. Six of the squadron's pilots led by deputy operations officer Lieutenant Edwards Park took delivery of a batch of six P-47Ds in Melbourne and flew them to Port Moresby on 1 January 1944. After conducting three hours more "transition training" there they then delivered them to Nadzab on 3 January 1944. By the end of the month all of its P-39N and Q model Airacobras had been reassigned to the 82ⁿᵈ and 110ᵗʰ Tactical Reconnaissance Squadrons in preparation for complete transition to Thunderbolts.

The 41ˢᵗ FS then took delivery of more new Thunderbolts, bolstered with inventory reassigned from the 348ᵗʰ FG. On 15 February 1944 it moved to Gusap, where it flew a limited number of missions, mostly ground attack, along New Guinea's northern coast from the Madang to Wewak areas. In July 1944 the 41ˢᵗ FS returned to Nadzab to re-equip the entire squadron with new natural metal finish P-47D-23s. Eight new natural metal finish Thunderbolts arrived at Nadzab from Melbourne on 1 July 1944 via Brisbane, Townsville, Horn Island and Port Moresby. This brought the squadron inventory to seventeen new Thunderbolts. A week later seven more were flown in, giving a total of 24.

The transition to the Thunderbolt was not smooth; in its first five weeks of operations the squadron lost ten Thunderbolts to various accidents including weather-related losses. By the time it left the theatre in August 1944 it had lost a total of nineteen Thunderbolts to accidents with only two lost in combat. The last loss in New Guinea occurred as late as 18 September 1944 when Flying Officer Denby Noble crashed into the water in bad visibility during a delivery flight from Townsville.

The 41ˢᵗ FS "Flying Buzzsaw" insignia was also used by the Oldsmobile company to promote war bonds.

Markings

Although allocated squadron numbers were applied in the 70 – 99 range, the 41ˢᵗ FS also used a unique batch of numbers from 170 to 177 for Yellow Flight, a carry-on from the Airacobra era. On paper Red Flight operated numbers in the 70s, White in the 80s and Blue in the 90s, however in practice these numbers were often mixed up for mission assignments. The cowls had a yellow asymmetric design painted on the front which varied on each airframe. Black piping was usually applied to this yellow design on both Olive Drab and natural metal finish airframes. Relatively few 41ˢᵗ FS Thunderbolts were named and decorated. With no dedicated squadron artist, most art was applied by ground crews or pilots. Neither the squadron nor its sister unit the 40ᵗʰ FS applied squadron numbers on the cowls.

41st Fighter Squadron

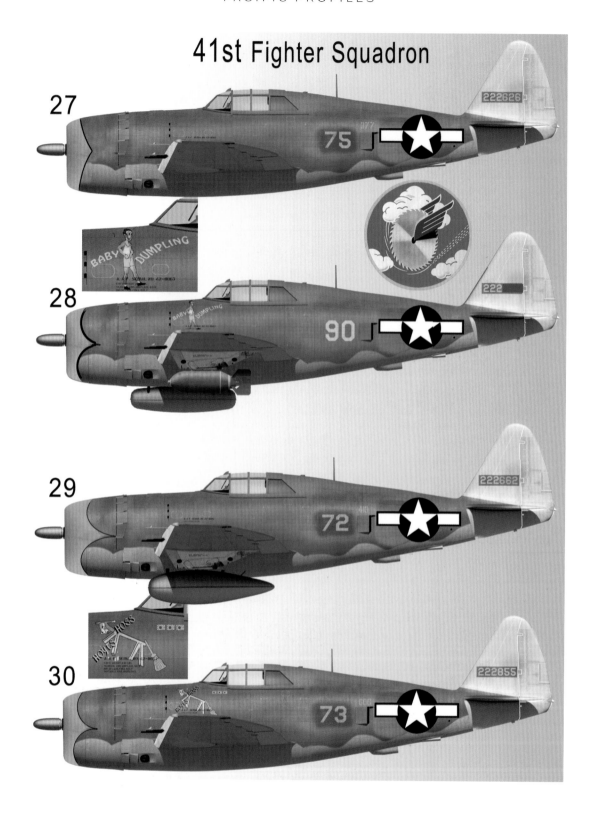

27

28

29

30

Profile 27: P-47D-3 serial 42-22626, MSN 377, squadron number 75

Assembled at the Commonwealth Aircraft Corporation factory in Melbourne in November 1943, Lieutenant Erick Kyro of Red Flight most often flew this airframe.

Profile 28: P-47D-3 serial 42-22*** (serial unknown), squadron number 90, *Baby Dumpling*

It is unclear who named this Blue Flight Thunderbolt, however the fighter was named after a cartoon character in cartoonist Chic Young's long-running comic strip *Blondie* which commenced in 1930. The strip narrated the life and times of the Bumstead family whose first baby was named Alexander, nicknamed Baby Dumpling.

Profile 29: P-47D-3 serial 42-22662, MSN 413, squadron number 72

This P-47D was assembled at the Commonwealth Aircraft Corporation factory in Melbourne in November 1943. On 14 February 1944 Lieutenant John Hartsfield of Red Flight left formation with a smoking engine and baled out at low altitude behind Wewak while returning from a ground attack mission. His aircraft and body were identified after the war.

Profile 30: P-47D-11 serial 42-22855, MSN 606, squadron number 73, *Hoyt's Hoss*

Named by Lieutenant Edward Hoyt of Red Flight, this Thunderbolt was reassigned to the 58th FG when the 41st FS left the theatre. Hoyt's nickname was "Judge", and he was later promoted to captain. The art work depicts a hobby horse made out of a work bench.

P-47D-3 Baby Dumpling, the subject of Profile 28, at Gusap.

41st Fighter Squadron

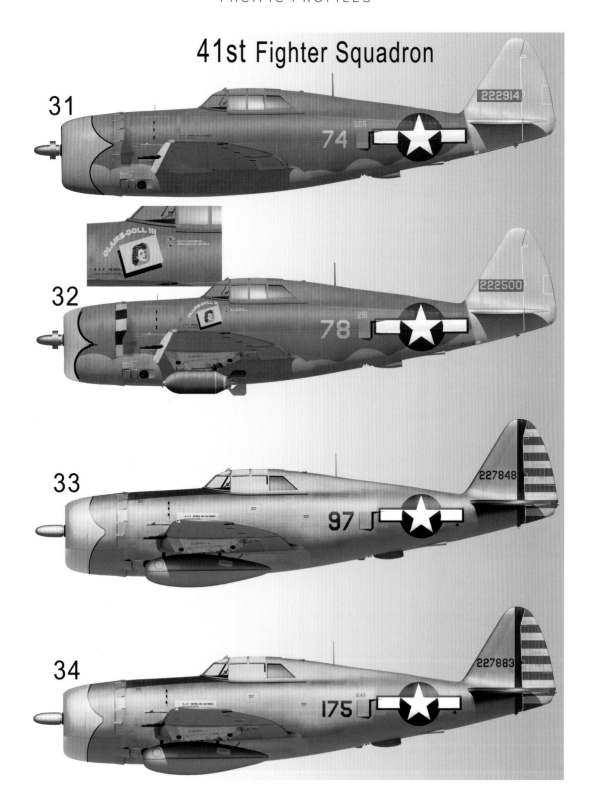

31

32

33

34

Profile 31: P-47D-11 serial 42-22914, MSN 665, squadron number 74

This Thunderbolt was collected in Melbourne at the end of 1943, before arriving in Port Moresby on 1 January 1944 via Townsville. It was flown to Nadzab on 3 January 1944 by 41st FS deputy operations officer Lieutenant Edwards Park. It was destroyed on 12 February 1944 when Captain Nelson ran off the end of Gusap's runway. It was replaced by 42-22929, another P-47D-11 which was also allocated squadron number 74.

Profile 32: P-47D-2 serial 42-22500, MSN 251, squadron number 78, *Claire Doll III*

Assigned to and named by Lieutenant Raymond Weidmeyer, this Thunderbolt was assigned into the 41st FS at Nadzab from the 310th FS around June 1944. It retained the latter unit's black and yellow cowls. Note that squadron number 78 is not confirmed from photographic evidence, rather Red Flight's sequential operations logs indicate this likely number.

Profile 33: P-47D-23 serial 42-27848, MSN 1510, (possibly squadron number 97)

On 4 August 1944 a training flight of sixteen new natural metal finish Thunderbolts was led over the New Guinea highlands by Captain Carl Bohman from Nadzab Strip #3. The formation was returning to Nadzab from Bena Bena when it encountered thick cloud and heavy turbulence near Dumpu at around 12,000 feet. Bohman's lead Blue Flight comprised three other pilots: Lieutenants Henry Frintner, Robert Gustavson and Raby Jeannes. Fourteen Thunderbolts returned to Nadzab at 1645, however Bohman and Frintner remain MIA. Note the squadron number of the Thunderbolt Bohman was flying as depicted here is not confirmed; 97 is a sequential guess sourced from the allocation of new squadron numbers for Blue Flight.

Profile 34: P-47D-23 serial 42-27883, MSN 1545, squadron number 175

This natural metal finish Thunderbolt was allocated squadron number 175, one of the unique sequential series of numbers from 170 to 177 for Yellow Flight. This was a legacy system preferred by Airacobra pilots who had been previously allocated the same numbers for their Airacobras.

Seen at Gusap, Sue-Anne II was P-47D-11 serial 42-22643 which was written off on 2 February 1944 at Nadzab when Captain Carey Wooley hit a tree after experienced engine failure during take-off.

P-47D-3 serial 42-22662, as depicted in Profile 29, tries to make it home after receiving damage from anti-aircraft fire over Wewak.

Lieutenant Raymond Weidmeyer with P-47D-2 serial 42-22500, the subject of Profile 32, at Nadzab

CHAPTER 7
69th Fighter Squadron "The Fightin' 69th"

The 69th FS was one of three which fell under the command umbrella of the 58th Fighter Group led by Lieutenant Colonel Gwen Atkinson. Squadron commander Captain Milton Self took the 69th FS to New Guinea. A handful of pilots including Self were attached to the 348th FG at Port Moresby for combat experience in late 1943. These pilots flew the 58th FG's first combat mission on 17 December 1943 alongside 348th FG Thunderbolts in a fierce combat with about 30 Japanese fighters over New Britain's Arawe peninsula. A total of eleven kills was claimed by the Thunderbolts, however in fact only one Japanese fighter was lost: a 59th *Sentai* Ki-43-II flown by Lieutenant Masuzawa Masanao. Two of the claims were made by 69th FS pilots Lieutenant Francis Donar and Captain Howard Tuman, both of whom had been in the theatre only a few days. These attached pilots soon returned to Brisbane from where they commenced aerial deliveries of new P-47D-16 Thunderbolts to Port Moresby via Rockhampton and Horn Island.

The 69th FS headquarters was established at Horanda 'drome, Dobodura, on 29 December 1943, with the aim of moving the entire 58th FG to Cape Gloucester early in the New Year. However this objective was cancelled when it was discovered that the captured airfield would not hold the heavy weight of the Thunderbolt. Instead, all three squadrons would wait at Dobodura pending the completion of Saidor. The 69th FS's first mission departed Dobodura and comprised four Thunderbolts which scrambled to locate an unidentified aircraft approaching Buna on 17 February 1944. However, the scramble proved to be a false alarm.

The 69th FS moved to Saidor in early April, and then on 19 April the first Thunderbolt fighter-bomber mission was flown which attacked Japanese supplies at Cape Croiselles, north of Madang. The squadron's ground echelon left Saidor by ship in mid-August, leaving the theatre bound for Noemfoor in Dutch New Guinea. However, flight operations continued at Saidor until early September 1944. The 69th FS had limited chance to engage with enemy aircraft as Wewak was all but abandoned by mid-February 1944. Instead, the unit confined itself to escort and low-level attack missions.

The 69th FS lost nineteen Thunderbolts in New Guinea, however only one was combat-related. This was when Lieutenant George Wood was shot down near Wewak on 29 May 1944 by anti-aircraft fire. The non-combat losses were due to various other causes including mechanical failure, bad weather, mid-air collisions and landing and take-off accidents.

The 69th FS logo was approved in June 1942, described as "on sky blue disc, a mailed cubit arm issuing from a base and grasping a torch of gold, all in front of a lightning bolt issuing from a white cloud formation". It was replaced after the war by a "Werewolves" logo.

Markings

After arriving in New Guinea it was determined at group level that the 58th FG's Thunderbolts would retain the squadron alphabetical prefix they had used in the US: the 69th FS kept letter "A", the 310th FS "H" and the 311th FS "V". Allocated 69th FS numbers lay in the A1 to A33 range, and further identification was provided by painting cowls white, with the cowl's top half left Olive Drab to reduce glare for the pilot. Although the squadron had used red as a unit colour back in the US, it was decided to change this to white in New Guinea for security reasons. Later on in the Philippines it reverted back to red.

P-47D-15 serial 42-23224 Sleepy Time Gal, the subject of Profile 39, at Saidor.

Thunderbolt Gilda Jean at Horanda 'drome whose serial number is unknown.

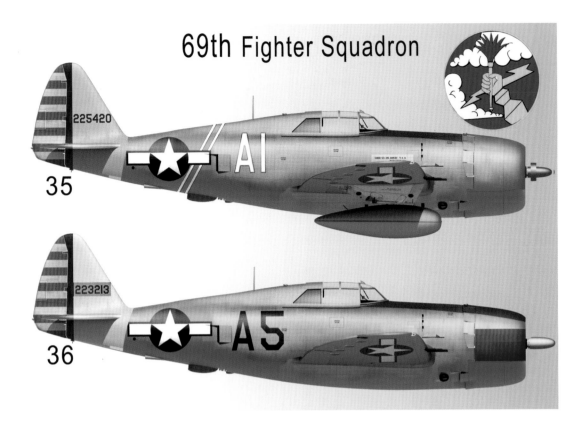

Profile 35: P-47D-20 serial 42-25420, MSN 997, squadron identifier A1

Squadron commander Major Milton Self (recently promoted from captain) chose the first squadron identifier to designate his leadership position on this natural metal finish Thunderbolt. The fighter is illustrated as it appeared during the first few weeks of operations, without its nose art. It was later lost in the Philippines on 22 January 1945 when flown by Lieutenant Donald Fish.

Profile 36: P-47D-15 serial 42-23213, MSN 964, squadron identifier A5

This airframe was stripped back to natural metal finish around mid-1944 just before it left the New Guinea theatre. The fighter is illustrated with its cowl marked with a red wide cowl stripe, just before it departed for Dutch New Guinea, which was a reversion to the original 69th FS colour.

69th Fighter Squadron

Profile 37: P-47D-15 serial 42-23152, MSN 903, squadron identifier A5, *Golden Gopher*

On 18 May 1944 Captain Harry McMullen abandoned this aircraft about twelve miles from the mouth of the Ramu River, on return to Saidor following a strafing mission against Wewak. His engine was hit over the target by anti-aircraft fire, and he baled out. After being spotted in a clearing, McMullen was instructed to clear a grass field landing ground so he could be rescued. On 29 May 1944 fellow pilot Lieutenant Guy Johnson borrowed an army L-4 Cub at Saidor and flew to Madang where he refueled and over-nighted. Next day he put down in the sparse field, but it proved too short for a safe departure. After further clearing the Cub successfully got airborne the following day and returned to Saidor. The original serial was painted over and re-applied in black, and the fighter is illustrated carrying a 1,000-pound general purpose bomb.

Profile 38: P-47D-2 serial 42-8129, MSN 277, squadron identifier A30

This Thunderbolt was reassigned into the 69th FS from the 342nd FS, becoming one of the first to enter service with the 58th FG at Saidor. Note the top yellow cowl flap and the outlined orange canopy.

Profile 39: P-47D-15 serial 42-23224, MSN 975, squadron identifier A23, *Sleepy Time Gal*

This Thunderbolt was assigned into the 69th FS at Saidor. Note the yellow lining on the bottom canopy and the semi-circular masking on the bottom of the white fin. The original serial number was painted over and re-applied in black. The art was a direct copy of a calendar girl artwork similarly titled by artist Alberto Vargas.

Profile 40: P-47D-20 serial 42-25400, MSN 977, squadron identifier A23, *Sleepy Time Gal*

This fighter was a replacement for the original *Sleepy Time Gal* when it was retired from service. Note the original cowl with the nose-art was kept and it was remarked with a black stripe through the name.

A brand-new natural metal finish 69th FS P-47D-23 at Nadzab in June 1944.

Nose art on a P-47D at Saidor, aptly named for the 69th FS.

P-47D-20 serial 42-25400 Sleepy Time Gal, the subject of Profile 40, at Noemfoor just after it left New Guinea. It is fitted with the paint-stripped cowl from Profile 39, with modified nose art.

CHAPTER 8
310th Fighter Squadron

The 310th FS was one of three which fell under the command umbrella of the 58th Fighter Group led by Lieutenant Colonel Gwen Atkinson, the other two being the 69th and 311th FS. Squadron commander Major Jack McClure Jr took the 310th FS to New Guinea, replaced on 27 April 1944 by Captain Donald Booty.

The air contingent took delivery at Eagle Farm near Brisbane of 21 new P-47D-16s in early February 1944 for aerial delivery to New Guinea. On 13 February they flew from Brisbane to Mackay for refueling, then on to Townsville. The following day they flew to Cairns, where after a few days they flew to Port Moresby on 18 February via Horn Island for refueling. The following day they flew over the Owen Stanley Ranges to Dobodura.

At Dobodura several new airframes were redistributed among the group's other two squadrons, allocating the 310th FS a total of two dozen Thunderbolts. These were structured into Flights A, B and C, each of seven aircraft, with one spare Thunderbolt per flight. On 25 February Captain Lester Wolf led sixteen fighters on the squadron's first combat mission, a patrol over an area north of Cape Gloucester on New Britain where US amphibious landing operations were still underway.

On 8 March the 310th FS received orders to move to Saidor, and the ground echelon commenced packing to do so by ship. Meanwhile the air echelon staged through Nadzab from where it conducted several escort missions throughout the rest of March. On 23 March Captain Lester Wolf led sixteen of the squadron's Thunderbolts on their first extended fighter sweep, however no enemy were encountered. On 3 April the squadron's Thunderbolts flew to Saidor to set up their new base. Six nuisance raids in the period from 11 through 18 March by Japanese Ki-48 light bombers interrupted camp life. On 8 April the 310th FS escorted medium bombers on a strike against Wewak and Tadji airfields. Soon afterwards its Thunderbolts started a series of ground attack missions against Japanese supply areas along the New Guinea coast, with each Thunderbolt toting two 500-pound bombs.

The 310th FS's ground echelon left Saidor by ship in mid-August bound for Noemfoor in Dutch New Guinea, however Thunderbolt operations continued at Saidor until early September 1944. In the end, the squadron had no chance to engage with enemy fighters as Wewak had been all but abandoned by mid-February 1944.

The 310th FS lost thirteen Thunderbolts while in New Guinea, all due to non-combat causes. The most unusual loss occurred on 14 June 1944 when Captain Charles Cracey departed Saidor for a flight test in fine weather just after lunch. He was never seen nor heard from again.

The 310th FS logo was a blue disc with two lightning bolts surmounted with a skull, adorned with a top hat supported by a bow tie and pair of dice, all within a narrow yellow border. The blue represents the sky, the yellow refers to the sun and the excellence required of air force personnel. The skull represents death and the possibility that the unit may be called to defend peace at any time. The dice symbolizes that the squadron will win with a six in its gamble with death. The lightning bolts denote weapons.

Markings

It was determined at group level after arriving in New Guinea that the 58th FG's Thunderbolts would retain the alphabetical prefix they had used in the US to assist with squadron identification: the 310th FS was already using letter "H", the 69th FS "A" and the 311th FS "V". Allocated squadron identifiers lay in the H34 to H66 range, and further identification was provided by painting cowls yellow. The squadron had colourful nose art, some with sophisticated designs. Considerable confusion has arisen from interpreting these yellow cowls as white in certain types of monochromatic film, thus misidentifying squadron Thunderbolts as those of the 311th FS and *vice versa*.

P-47D-16 serial 42-75955 Munchkin, the subject of Profile 41, at Nadzab.

The 310th FS had the most lavish cowls of the 58th FG's three squadrons. Archy the Cockroach III is seen at Saidor in April 1944.

Another 310th FS beauty was Pioneer Peggy seen here at Saidor.

P-47D-16 serial 42-76059, the subject of Profile 43, at Saidor shortly prior to its loss in April 1944.

310th Fighter Squadron

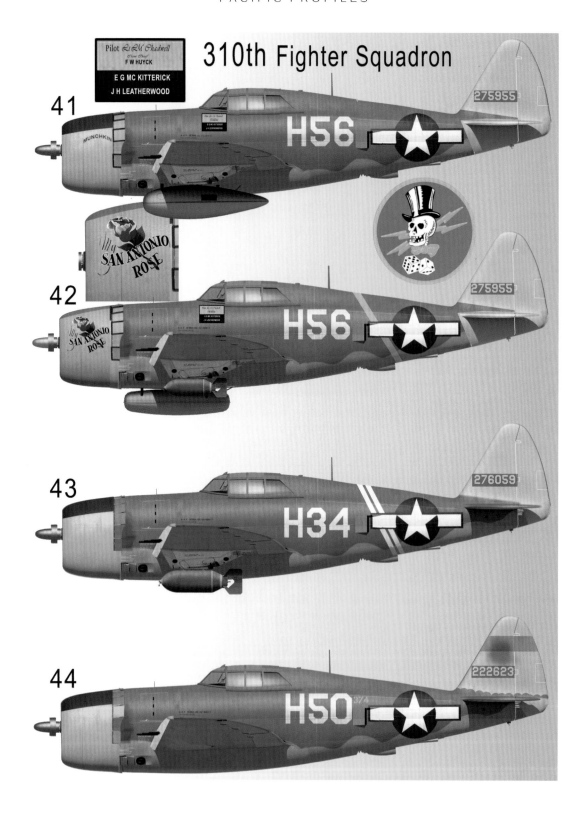

Profiles 41 & 42: P-47D-16 serial 42-75955, MSN 4306, squadron identifier H56, *Munchkin / My San Antonio Rose*

P-47D *Munchkin* was the assigned as the mount of Texan Lieutenant Leroy Chadwell, with Staff Sergeant Frank Huyck as crew chief. *Munchkin* was the endearing nickname Chadwell gave to his girlfriend, but he changed the art to *My San Antonio Rose* after she sent him a "Dear John" letter. The fighter was removed from the flightline following an operational accident with Lieutenant John Ahern at Saidor on 19 April 1944. Profile 41 illustrates the aircraft at Horanda 'drome just after it was received by Chadwell. Profile 42 shows it toting a 500-pound bomb and "Brisbane Tank", with the new cowl art and a single yellow stripe after Chadwell was made flight leader. The surnames Kitternick and Leatherwood in the names panel are those of the two assistant ground crew.

Profile 43: P-47D-16 serial 42-76059, MSN 4410, squadron identifier H34

With double stripes indicating his role as squadron commander, this new Thunderbolt was flown by assigned pilot Major Jack McClure Jr into Dobodura on 19 February 1944. It was lost about a month later on 11 April about ten miles southwest of Madang when borrowed by Lieutenant Clement Theed Jr to assist a search for three 311th FS Thunderbolts shot down earlier that day. When flying low at 400 feet during the search, the flight leader noticed that the fourth aircraft flown by Theed had crashed and was burning, the cause of which remains unknown.

Profile 44: P-47D-3 serial 42-22623, MSN 374, squadron identifier H50

Assembled at the Commonwealth Aircraft Corporation factory near Melbourne in November 1943, this Thunderbolt served briefly with the 341st FS before transfer to the 310th FS at Saidor via a service squadron around April 1944. The fighter is illustrated shortly after it was received into the squadron. It retained the previous yellow tail band from 341st FS days, however the previous squadron number 37 on the tail was painted out.

A colour slide of the nose art on P-47D-16 serial 42-75955 My San Antonio Rose, the subject of Profile 42.

310th Fighter Squadron

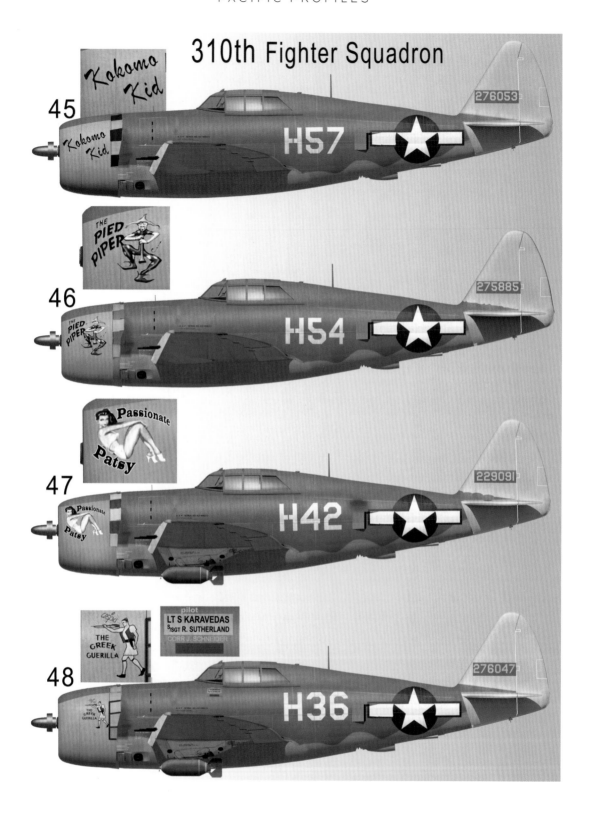

45

46

47

48

Profile 45: P-47D-16 serial 42-76053, MSN 4404, squadron identifier H57, *Kokomo Kid*

Lieutenant Crystal Andress badly damaged this fighter during a landing accident at Nadzab on 20 March 1944. It was turned over to a service squadron for repairs however it is unclear whether it was returned to service. The fighter was named after the town of Kokomo in Indiana.

Profile 46: P-47D-16 serial 42-75885, MSN 4236, squadron identifier H54, *The Pied Piper*

This Thunderbolt was assembled at the Commonwealth Aircraft Corporation factory near Melbourne in January 1944. The marking line at the bottom of the fin indicates the fin was painted white with a brush rather than spray-painted. Note the truncated calligraphy of the "5" in H54.

Profile 47: P-47D-16 serial 42-29091, MSN 2753, squadron identifier H42, *Passionate Patsy*

This Thunderbolt became one of the 310th FS's longest-serving aircraft and its decorative cowl was later transferred to a P-47N "bubbletop" in the Philippines. Note the orange cowl flaps rather than the usual yellow. The fighter is illustrated toting a 500-pound bomb.

Profile 48: P-47D-16 serial 42-76047, MSN 4398, squadron identifier H36, *The Greek Guerilla*

This Thunderbolt was assigned to Lieutenant Spiros Karavedas, who was proud of his Greek ancestry. The nose art featured a Greek soldier yelling "Aera", the war cry used during the Greek confrontation war against German and Italian forces on the Northern Epirus front from 1940 to April 1941. The other side of the cowling was named *Gladys* by crew chief Staff Sergeant Robert Sutherland after his girlfriend.

P-47D-16 serial 42-76053 Kokomo Kid, as depicted in Profile 45, at Noemfoor in Dutch New Guinea just after leaving the main New Guinea theatre.

Lieutenant Robert Powell at Saidor in August 1944 with P-47D-21 Meanie, as shown in Profile 49.

CHAPTER 9
311ᵗʰ Fighter Squadron

The 311ᵗʰ FS was one of three which fell under the command umbrella of the 58ᵗʰ Fighter Group led by Lieutenant Colonel Gwen Atkinson, the other two being the 69ᵗʰ and 310ᵗʰ FS. Major Landis Carter took the squadron to Australia and New Guinea but on 12 February 1944 he was transferred to Fifth Bomber Command. His replacement was Captain Harry "Oddie" Oldren who was promoted to major several months later.

The 311ᵗʰ FS headquarters was established at Horanda 'drome, Dobodura, on 29 December 1943, with the intention of moving the entire 58ᵗʰ FG to Cape Gloucester early in the New Year. However, the move was cancelled when it was discovered that the recently captured airfield could not hold the heavy weight of the Thunderbolt. Instead, all three squadrons were ordered to wait at Dobodura pending the completion of Saidor.

The squadron ferried its aircraft from Australia to New Guinea in several ferry flights. The last departed Eagle Farm on 20 January 1944 comprising eight fighters led by Captain Don Jander, but bad weather delayed their arrival at Horn Island until 25 January. An attempt to reach Port Moresby turned back on 29 January and the next day the same attempt was made this time with a B-25 to lead them as a navigation ship. The Thunderbolts became separated from the B-25 but all but two found Port Moresby. These two landed wheels-up on Yule Island, on the south coast of Papua and about 100 miles from Port Moresby.

The 311ᵗʰ FS's first mission was to escort C-47 transports to Saidor and comprised eight Thunderbolts which departed Dobodura on 2 February led by 58ᵗʰ FG operations officer Major Thomas Klemovich. Three P-47s abandoned the mission due to engine troubles and were escorted back to Finschhafen by a fourth. In the Saidor circuit area a fifth experienced complete engine failure and made a dead-stick landing. By the end of February 1944, the 311ᵗʰ FS had 25 Thunderbolts on charge.

On 8 March the 311ᵗʰ FS received orders to move to Saidor, and the ground echelon had soon moved there mostly by ship. Meanwhile the air echelon staged through Nadzab from where it conducted several escort missions throughout the rest of March. On Easter Sunday, 8 April 1944, the squadron escorted medium bombers on a strike against Wewak and Tadji airfields.

On 11 April, and contrary to intelligence reports that Japanese fighters would not be encountered over Wewak, sixteen Hollandia-based Ki-43-II *Hayabusa* and eight Ki-61 *Hien* patrolled the region. Led by 33ʳᵈ *Sentai* commander Captain Namai Kiyoshi, these fighters attacked the incoming USAAF fighter contingent including fifteen 311ᵗʰ FS Thunderbolts. These had been escorting Mitchells at medium altitude, but the Japanese fighters dove into them. The first loss was *Fascinatin' Phil* flown by Lieutenant Marvin Rothman which crashed into foothills behind Boram airfield. The other two losses were Lieutenant Bill Graham and Major Thomas Bullington, the latter of which had pleaded to go on the mission despite being due for leave.

Both Graham and Bullington's *Cowtown Cyclone* were last seen heading southeast, with both shot down near Wewak. The Japanese claimed twelve "definite" Thunderbolt kills from the encounter with five more uncertain, although only three Thunderbolts were lost, all from the 311th FS. Namai later reported that the battle had been "one-sided" in Japanese favour.

After this disastrous mission the 311th FS switched its focus to ground attack missions against supply areas along the New Guinea coast, often toting a pair of 500-pound bombs, one under each wing. The squadron's ground echelon left Saidor by ship in mid-August, leaving the theatre bound for Noemfoor in Dutch New Guinea, although flight operations continued at Saidor until early September 1944. The 311th FS lost eighteen Thunderbolts in New Guinea, three being combat-related. All of the other losses were due to various other causes including mechanical failure, bad weather, one mid-air collision and landing and take-off accidents.

The 311th FS logo was a coiled snake bearing fangs which represents the unit's mission to strike swiftly. The cartridge belt reflects the integral part of any mission, while the two shades of blue reflect the ability to operate at any time, in any weather. The yellow colour of the cartridge belt refers to the sun and the excellence required of air force personnel.

Markings

After arriving in New Guinea, it was determined at group level that the 58th FG's Thunderbolts would retain the squadron alphabetical prefixes they had used in the US to assist with aerial identification: the 311th FS was using the letter "V", the 69th FS "A" and the 310th FS "H". Allocated squadron identifiers lay in the V67 to V99 range, and further identification was provided by painting cowl side panels blue, with the cowl's top half left Olive Drab to reduce glare for the pilot.

The 311th FS commenced operations with hand-me-downs from the 348th FG including the second *Fiery Ginger III* (see Profile 78) flown by Lieutenant Anthony Kupferer for his first three missions in early February 1944 from Horanda 'drome. These Thunderbolts already had white tails and the first nose art was applied on 16 February at Horanda, including *Cowtown Cyclone*, the first Thunderbolt to be decorated. There was an unspoken convention that the pilot could decorate the cowl's left-hand side, and the crew chief the other.

Lieutenant James O'Leary (right) at Saidor in April 1944 with P-47D-11 serial 42-23235 Strictly From Brooklyn, as depicted Profile 54.

Profile 49: P-47D-21 serial 43-25626, MSN 1203, squadron identifier V68, *Meanie*

This natural metal finish Thunderbolt was assigned to Lieutenant Robert Powell at Saidor in July 1944. Powell had played in the undefeated 1939 Wolverine football team in Michigan, and after graduating as an aircraft engineer in late 1942 had joined the Aviation Cadet Program. After being commissioned and earning his pilot wings, he completed combat training on the P-47D and was assigned to the 311th FS which he accompanied to Brisbane. Powell was temporarily attached to the 348th FG at Port Moresby to obtain combat experience. Shortly after leaving New Guinea, Powell ditched this Thunderbolt off Batanta Island in the Netherlands East Indies along with seven others (including Profile 54) on 21 October 1944 when the formation became lost in weather. Note that the code V68 is deduced from sequential squadron assignments and requires confirmation.

Profile 50: P-47D-21 serial 43-25634, MSN 1211, squadron identifier V69

This natural metal finish Thunderbolt was assigned to Lieutenant Art Marston and crew chief Staff Sergeant Ben Bridgers at Saidor in July 1944. Captain Don Jander wrote off the fighter at Noemfoor on 11 September 1944, shortly after leaving the main New Guinea theatre. Marston had the hula girl copied from a magazine, while it was Bridgers' idea to paint the cowl doors white.

311th Fighter Squadron

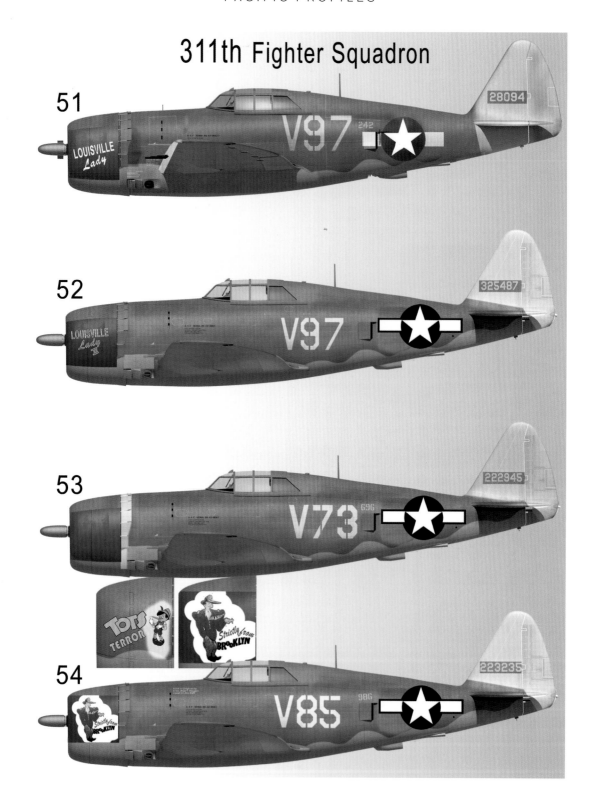

Profile 51: P-47D-2 serial 42-8094, MSN 242, squadron identifier V97, *Louisville Lady*

Received from the 348th FG, this early series Thunderbolt was assigned to pilot Lieutenant Anthony Kupferer. Lieutenant Ray Evans flew this fighter on 2 February 1944, when eight of the 311th FS's Thunderbolts flew the 58th FG's first combat mission. It was transferred to the Combat Replacement Training Center (see Profile 91) when a new batch of Thunderbolts was received by the squadron. It was replaced by a P-47D-21 (see Profile 52). The fighter is illustrated as it appeared at Saidor just prior to its transfer from the 311th FS.

Profile 52: P-47D-21 serial 43-25487, MSN 3362, squadron identifier V97, *Louisville Lady II*

This airframe was among the last batch of D-21s to leave the factory in Olive Drab finish. Following a strike against supplies near Alexishafen on 28 August 1944, flown by Lieutenant Anthony Kupferer, it collided mid-air with *Billy Boy* flown by Lieutenant William Ritter. Both pilots baled out safely and were rescued by an Australian destroyer.

Profile 53: P-47D-11 serial 42-22945 MSN 696, squadron identifier V73

Assigned to crew chief Sergeant Erich Rohrken, the history of this fighter is unclear although there is no record of its loss to an accident or in combat. It is referenced to an early photo taken at Saidor without nose art, however it is possible the fighter was later named and/or decorated.

Profile 54: P-47D-11 serial 42-23235, MSN 986, squadron identifier V85, *Strictly From Brooklyn / Tot's Terror*

Pilot Lieutenant James O'Leary first named this fighter *Strictly From Brooklyn* at Saidor. After he returned to the US it was taken over by Lieutenant Jack Brown who was flight leader for C Flight, and who renamed it *Tot's Terror*. Brown ditched this Thunderbolt off Batanta Island in the Netherlands East Indies along with seven others (including Profile 49) on 21 October 1944 when the formation became lost in weather.

An unidentified crew chief in the cockpit of Strictly From Brooklyn at Saidor in April 1944 with the 311th FS mascot puppy.

P-47D Lanky Yankee at Noemfoor in late 1944. This was a previous 69th FS P-47D-15 or -16 which also had blue stripes painted on the Olive Drab rudder in addition to the blue band on the cowl.

There was no shortage of quality artwork for the 311th FS Thunderbolts, however Gloria's identity remains elusive.

P-47D-11 serial 42-75332, squadron number V68, at Saidor in February 1944, with no blue cowl. The same squadron number was later allocated to a natural metal finish P-47D-21, as illustrated in Profile 49.

A pair of 311th FS P-47D-23s receive maintenance in the Philippines. A series of black bands attended a revised markings system, alongside the eradication of the V-code markings. Philippines theatre markings involve a completely different set of parameters to those used earlier in the New Guinea Theatre.

P-47D-2 serial 42-8077, as depicted in Profile 57, at Seven-Mile with its signature red piping around the modified national insignia.

P-47D serial 42-8070, squadron number 6, seen at Nadzab #3 in May 1944.

CHAPTER 10
340th Fighter Squadron "The Minute Men"

The first Thunderbolts to arrive in New Guinea did so on 14 July 1943: 25 were flown up from Australia via Cairns and Horn Island led by 348th FG commander Lieutenant Colonel Neel Kearby. Nearly half of the contingent was from the 340th FS led by Captain Charles McDonald. The squadron initially set up at Seven-Mile 'drome in Port Moresby from where it commenced a series of familiarisation and C-47 escort missions to Wau and Marilinen. During its first two months at Port Moresby it lost five airframes to accidents, incurring one fatality. On 13 December 1943 all three of the group's squadrons, the 340th, 341st and 342nd FS, were ordered to move to Finschhafen. The 340th FS later took up station at Saidor on 13 March 1944, then Nadzab #3 briefly before it left New Guinea for Wakde in Dutch New Guinea on 26 May 1944.

On the morning of 16 October 1943, the 340th FS alongside the 342nd FS escorted B-25s on a low-level attack mission against Alexishafen. The 340th FS was at 9,000 feet when they were attacked from above by Ki-61 *Hien* and Ki-43 *Hayabusa* fighters, which passed directly through the Thunderbolt shield and downed three Mitchells. On 3 February 1944 the 340th FS was one of several USAAF fighter units protecting a large formation of Liberators and Mitchells attacking Wewak. The Thunderbolts claimed eight of a total of fifteen kills made by USAAF fighters yet only one Japanese was lost: a 248th *Sentai* Ki-43 *Hayabusa* flown by Lieutenant Koga Keiji.

Captain Charles McDonald was replaced as squadron commander on 1 October 1943 by Major Hervey Carpenter, who was subsequently replaced by Captain Max Wiecks on 30 April 1944. The 340th FS lost a total of fourteen Thunderbolts in New Guinea, with no combat-related losses. All were due to various other causes including mechanical failure, a mid-air collision between two of the squadron's fighters near Finschhafen on 18 February 1944, and numerous landing and take-off accidents. The 340th FS moved to Wakde in Dutch New Guinea in late May 1944.

The 340th FS logo was approved on 27 March 1943, comprising a cartoon character in togs and brown helmet seated on a yellow lightning bolt, and firing a Tommy gun.

Markings

Upon arriving in Australia, it was determined at group level that the 340th FS would be assigned numerical identifiers from 1 to 25, with red maintained as the squadron colour. Red tail tips started appearing a few weeks after operations began at Port Moresby, with the squadron number stencilled in red on the white fin. This system was replaced around early 1944 by a red band applied on the mid-tail section with the squadron number stencilled in white. This system continued with the first natural metal finish P-47D-20s and P-47D-23s which started arriving in the inventory at Nadzab #3 in early June 1944. In the case of natural metal finish airframes, the squadron number was applied in black or masked out to leave the number appearing underneath in natural metal finish.

340th Fighter Squadron

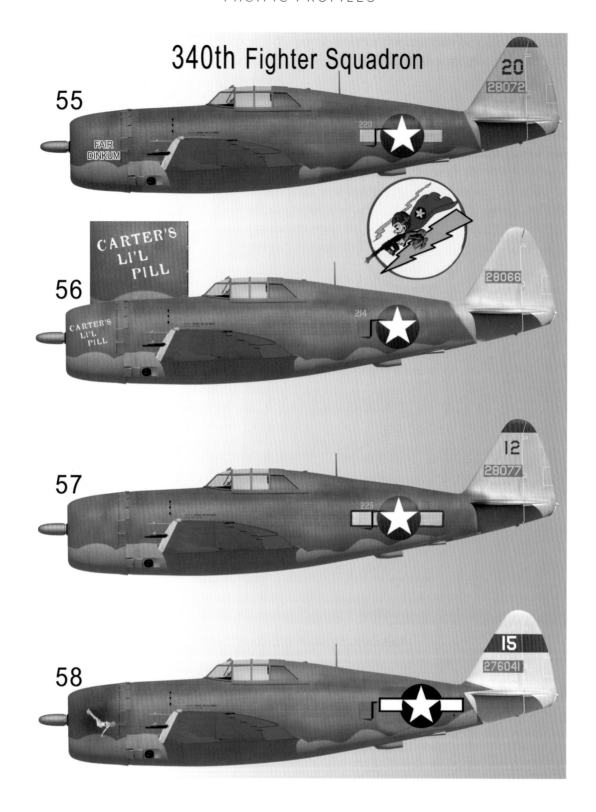

55

FAIR
DINKUM

20
28072

220

56

CARTER'S
LI'L
PILL

CARTER'S
LI'L
PILL

28066

214

57

12
28077

225

58

15
276041

Profile 55: P-47D-2 serial 42-8072, MSN 220, squadron number 20, *Fair Dinkum*

The phrase "fair dinkum" is Australian vernacular meaning something is genuine or real, and is still in common use today. This fighter suffered a bad landing accident on 28 September 1943 at Nadzab but was repaired and returned to service.

Profile 56: P-47D-2 serial 42-8066, MSN 214, *Carter's Li'l Pill*

Lieutenant William Carter took delivery of this Thunderbolt at Eagle Farm, Brisbane, on 15 July 1943. Following familiarisation flights, he flew it as part of the 340th FS's move to New Guinea to Townsville on 22 July, then via Cooktown and Horn Island before arriving at Seven-Mile 'drome, Port Moresby, two days later. The fighter is profiled as it arrived at Port Moresby, without a squadron number or red tail tip. For security reasons, the tailplane had already been painted white for the journey.

Carter named the fighter *Carter's Li'l Pill* in Australia as a rejoinder between his surname and a popular and widely advertised medicine of the time "Carter's Little Liver Pills". He flew the fighter for the next two months mainly escorting C-47s on supply runs. On 1 October 1943 Lieutenant Wallace Harding borrowed the fighter for a training flight but suffered an oil pump failure on the way back to Seven-Mile 'drome, causing the engine to seize. Harding forced-landed with his gear retracted in a shallow lake northwest of Port Moresby near Waigani Swamp. The plane was undamaged in the landing, and Harding managed to walk to safety two days later. The fighter was salvaged post-war and is currently under restoration in Australia.

Profile 57: P-47D-2 serial 42-8077, MSN 225, squadron number 12

This Thunderbolt was the only one in the 348th FG which had red surround bars applied to the field-modified white bars, added to the single circular marking. The fighter is profiled as it appeared in September 1943.

Profile 58: P-47D-16 serial 42-76041, MSN 4392, squadron number 15

This Thunderbolt carried no name but was decorated with an Alberto Vargas girl taken from a 1943 calendar. Note this is an early example of the 1944-style red band applied mid-tail section with the squadron number stencilled in white.

Lieutenant William Carter at Seven-Mile 'drome with P-47D-2 Carter's Li'l Pill, as depicted in Profile 56.

340th Fighter Squadron

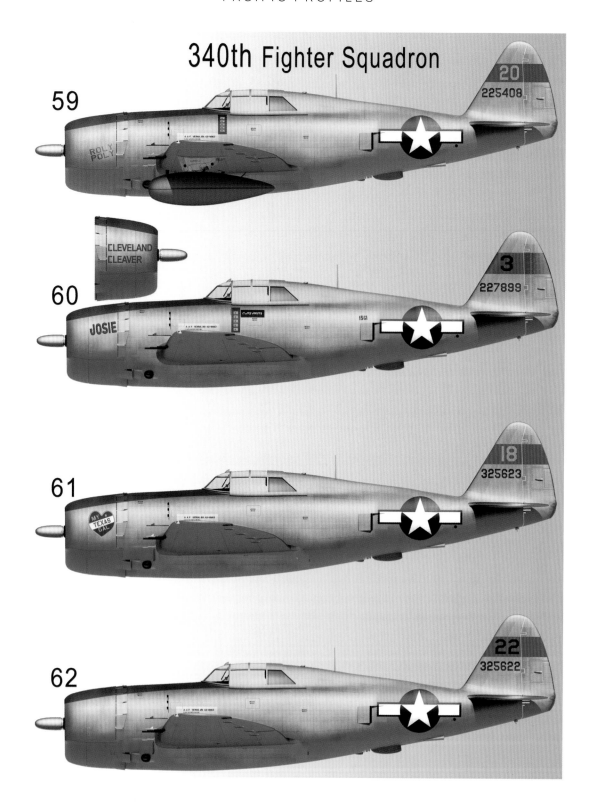

59

60

61

62

Profile 59: P-47D-20 serial 42-25408, MSN 3284, squadron number 20, *Roly Poly*

This fighter was assembled at the Commonwealth Aircraft Corporation factory in May 1944 and assigned to Lieutenant Myron Hnatio. The fighter is illustrated as it appeared in late June 1944 at Nadzab just before it proceeded with the 340th FS to Wakde in Dutch New Guinea. The squadron number 20 was masked off underneath the red band, retaining the natural metal finish.

Profile 60: P-47D-23 serial 42-27899, MSN 1561, squadron number 3, *Josie / Cleveland Cleaver*

P-47D-23 *Josie* was assigned to Lieutenant Michael "Mike" Dikovitsky at Nadzab in early June 1944. The fighter's crew chief, from Cleveland in Ohio, named the fighter *Cleveland Cleaver* on the other side of the cowl. This Thunderbolt subsequently served in the Philippines.

Profile 61: P-47D-21 serial 43-25623, MSN 3498, squadron number 18, *My Texas Gal*

This natural metal finish fighter was assigned to and named by Texan pilot Captain Andrew Lytle and was in fact his third "Texas Gal". The number 18 was masked off underneath the red band, retaining the natural metal finish. The heart motif appears in red, white and blue, the colours of the Texas flag. The later batches of -21 series left the factory in natural metal finish.

Profile 62: P-47D-23 serial 43-25622, MSN 3497, squadron number 22

This fighter was assigned into the 340th FS in June 1944 but was lost when an unidentified pilot baled out of it due to mechanical failure. It crashed into the side of a mountain about nine miles to the north of Nadzab, not far from Gain village.

The fin of P-47D-23 serial 43-25622, the subject of Profile 62, as it lies in jungle north of Nadzab.

The 340th FS flight line at Finschhafen in December 1943. In the foreground squadron number 21 has a forward-placed insignia with field-added white bars meaning it is either a P-47D-2 or early batch P-47D-3.

P-47D-20 serial 42-25408 Roly Poly, as depicted in Profile 59, at Nadzab in June 1944.

P-47D-23 serial 42-27899 Josie, the subject of Profile 60, as it appeared when serving in the Philippines.

Squadron number 15, a 340th FS Thunderbolt, flying over Nadzab.

Lieutenant John Lolos with the starboard cowl art on P-47D-3 serial 42-22607
Naughty Nadine (as depicted in Profile 63) at Dobodura in November 1943.

CHAPTER 11
341ˢᵗ Fighter Squadron "The Black Jacks"

The first Thunderbolts to arrive in New Guinea did so on 14 July 1943. Comprising a mixed batch of twenty five 348ᵗʰ FG fighters, nearly half of the contingent was from the 341ˢᵗ FS which moved its headquarters to Durand 'drome, Port Moresby, about a week later. From there it commenced a series of familiarisation and C-47 escort operations to Wau, Nadzab and Marilinen alongside the group's other two squadrons. On 13 December 1943 all three of the 348ᵗʰ FG squadrons were ordered to move to Finschhafen. The 341ˢᵗ FS later took up station at Saidor on 27 March 1944, then Nadzab #3 briefly before it left the main New Guinea theatre for Wakde in Dutch New Guinea on 22 May 1944. Major David Campbell took the 341ˢᵗ FS to New Guinea and was replaced by Major John Moore on 15 November 1943.

On 11 October 1943, 341ˢᵗ FS operations officer (and soon to be squadron commander and promoted to major) Captain John Moore was among a quartet of P-47s led by 348ᵗʰ FG commander Lieutenant Colonel Neel Kearby which undertook the first Thunderbolt mission over the Japanese base of Wewak. A total of nine victories was distributed between the Thunderbolts for which Kearby was later awarded the Medal of Honor. In fact, the Thunderbolts shot down only two Ki-43-IIs, but these were both high-profile officers being Captain Koyama Shigeru, commander of the 68ᵗʰ *Sentai*'s first squadron, and Lieutenant Colonel Teranishi Tamiya, the commander of the 14ᵗʰ Fighter Brigade.

On 7 November the 341ˢᵗ FS and the 342ⁿᵈ FS encountered particularly fierce resistance from Ki-43-II *Hayabusa* in a fight which spread from Nadzab to Saidor. The 341ˢᵗ FS shot down four *Hayabusa* against no Thunderbolt losses: 13ᵗʰ *Sentai* pilots Lieutenant Sakata Koichi and Sergeant Major Suzuki Sozaku together with Sergeant Toda Shiro of the 248ᵗʰ *Sentai* and Sergeant Shimanto Kikuo of the 59ᵗʰ *Sentai*.

On 1 December 1943 the 341ˢᵗ FS, alongside 36ᵗʰ FS Thunderbolts, escorted 90ᵗʰ BG Liberators to Wewak at medium altitude. Approaching the target, they were met by about 20 Ki-61 *Hien* and 30 Ki-43-II *Hayabusa* from the 59ᵗʰ and 248ᵗʰ *Sentai* in separate formations. With then escorts flying higher than the Liberators, there was a communications misunderstanding as to the formation's sequence and timing over the target. As a result, the rearwards bombers were attacked in a series of proficient and determined climbing attacks and three Liberators were downed.

The 341ˢᵗ FS incurred its first loss occurred at Cooktown, Australia, during a delivery flight when a new P-47D-2 was destroyed during a ground collision on 18 July 1943. The squadron lost a total of nineteen Thunderbolts in New Guinea, of which four were combat-related. The other fifteen were due to various causes including mechanical failure, bad weather, and landing and take-off accidents. Four of these losses were accidents at Durand 'drome. Poor fortune followed the 341ˢᵗ FS when Lieutenant Samuel Galik was killed in a landing accident during the ferry flight from Nadzab to Wakde on 4 June 1944, followed by the loss of squadron commander Major John Moore who was last seen in cloud near Ceram on 8 October 1944.

The 341st FS logo of an ace and jack of spades emulates its nickname of "The Black Jacks" acquired stateside during its training era.

Markings

Upon arriving in Australia, it was determined at group level that the 341st FS would be assigned numerical identifiers in the 26 to 50 range, with yellow maintained as squadron colour. Accordingly yellow tail tips were applied a few weeks after arriving at Durand, with the squadron number applied by a yellow stencil on the white fin. This system was replaced around early 1944 by a yellow band applied mid-tail section with the squadron number stencilled in white. This tail band system continued with the first natural metal finish P-47D-20s and P-47D-23s which started arriving in the inventory at Saidor in May 1944. In the case of natural metal finish airframes, the squadron number was applied in black (see Profile 70) or even masked out (see Profile 68), to leave a natural metal finish stencil. Wheel hubs were often decorated by ground crews.

P-47D-3 serial 42-22600 Oh Pudgy, as depicted in Profile 66, at Durand 'drome. Behind it with the modified white bar insignia is P-47D-2 serial 42-8130 Frankie, the subject of Profile 65.

Major Robert Rowland (centre) with his crew chief and assistant in front of P-47D-4 serial 42-22684 Miss Mutt II, as shown in Profile 67, at Finschhafen in February 1944.

Lieutenant John Lolos with P-47D-2 serial 42-8081 Hi Topper, the subject of Profile 71, at Durand around July 1943.

Major Robert Rowland's original fighter, P-47D-2 serial 42-8096 Miss Mutt, and predecessor to Miss Mutt II.

341st Fighter Squadron

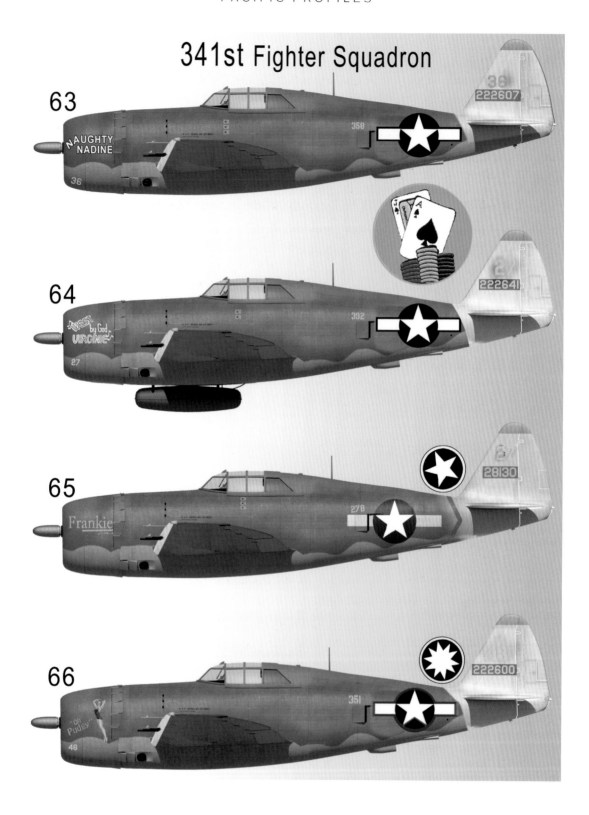

63

NAUGHTY NADINE

64

WEST by God VIRGINIE

65

Frankie

66

"ol' Pudgy"

Profile 63: P-47D-3 serial 42-22607, MSN 358, squadron number 36, *Naughty Nadine*

This fighter was assigned to both Lieutenants George Della and John Lolos at different times. The fighter had art on the starboard cowl as seen in the photo on page 78.

Profile 64: P-47D-3 serial 42-22641, MSN 392, squadron number 27, *West by God Virginie*

This Thunderbolt was assigned to and named by Captain Arthur Weeks with Staff Sergeant A Dorko as crew chief.

Profile 65: P-47D-2 serial 42-8130, MSN 278, squadron number 27, *Frankie*

Assigned to Lieutenant Sam Blair, this Thunderbolt was force-landed by an unknown pilot on an unknown date in November 1943 at the emergency field at Hood Point on the coast not far from Port Moresby. The fighter was abandoned, and its squadron number 27 was reassigned to P-47D-3 serial 42-22641 (see Profile 64). Note the line where the white tail had been masked off. The fighter had a US star insignia applied to its wheel hubs.

Profile 66: P-47D-3 serial 42-22600, MSN 351, squadron number 46, *Oh Pudgy*

This Thunderbolt retained its factory red outline on the star-and-bar. Note the unique multi-star wheel hub.

Captain Arthur Weeks with P-47D-3 serial 42-22641 West by God Virginie, the subject of Profile 64.

341st Fighter Squadron

Profile 67: P-47D-4 serial 42-22684, MSN 435, squadron number 31, *Miss Mutt II / Pride of Lodi, Ohio*

This Thunderbolt replaced the first *Miss Mutt*, P-47D-2 serial 42-8096, which was transferred out of the 341st FS for repairs. It was the mount of Major Robert Rowland from the township of Lodi who also named it *Pride of Lodi, Ohio*. Founded in 1811, Lodi is the oldest settlement in Medina County. The name of Lodi derives from northern Italy, where Napoleon won a battle in 1796. Note the Fifth Air Force logo wheel hubs.

Profile 68: P-47D-20 serial 42-25416, MSN 993, squadron number 31, *Miss Mutt III*

This Thunderbolt replaced the *Miss Mutt II* as depicted in Profile 67. It was the first natural metal finish Thunderbolt assigned to the 341st FS, and was allocated to Major Robert Rowland. The airframe sports the new design tail band, with the squadron number 31 masked off to leave a natural metal finish. Similar to its predecessor the fighter had the Fifth Air Force logo painted on the wheel hubs. The aircraft is illustrated with a 200-gallon drop-tank as used to ferry the 341st FS to Wakde in Dutch New Guinea in early June 1944 when the unit left the main New Guinea theatre.

Profile 69: P-47D-4 serial 42-22637, MSN 388, squadron number 38, *Daring Dottie III*

Assigned to squadron commander Major John Moore, this fighter is profiled as it appeared at Saidor in early 1944. The rear half of the airframe was stripped back to natural metal finish. Moore's previous Thunderbolt, *Daring Dottie II*, was transferred to the 342nd FS following repairs after an accident. His first *Daring Dottie* was the P-47C he trained on in the US.

Profile 70: P-47D-23 serial 42-27596, MSN 1258, squadron number 38, *Daring Dottie III*

This fighter was assigned to squadron commander Major John Moore at Saidor in May 1944 to replace P-47D-4 serial 42-22637 (see Profile 69), however his crew chief kept the cowl for sentimental reasons, thus retaining the name. This is the Thunderbolt in which Moore disappeared when he became lost in cloud near Ceram on 8 October 1944.

P-47D-20 serial 42-25416 Miss Mutt III, as depicted in Profile 68, is inspected at Saidor a few days after it was received by the 431st FS in May 1944.

341st Fighter Squadron

71

72

73

74

Profile 71: P-47D-2 serial 42-8081, MSN 229, squadron number 36, *Hi Topper*

Nicknamed *Hi Topper* by Lieutenant John Lolos to reflect that he flew high over cloud, the name and art appeared on both sides of the cowl. The fighter was lost on 10 October 1943 when Lolos departed Durand on a mission to escort C-47s to Nadzab. After approaching Port Moresby subsequent to the mission Lolos obtained permission to leave formation and test his guns at the offshore range near Redscar Bay. When strafing low some of his tracers ricocheted into the belly tank and caught fire. Lolos ditched the flaming fighter about three miles offshore but managed to secure the survival dinghy before the Thunderbolt sank. He was subsequently collected by an RAAF Catalina and taken to Port Moresby and then to Australia for hospitalisation. The fighter's wheel hubs were decorated with the spiral as illustrated.

Profile 72: P-47D-2 serial 42-8058, MSN 206, squadron number 28, *Battlin' Beaut*

This fighter was damaged in an operational accident at Dobodura on 8 October 1943. It was repaired and put back into service with a different wheel hub design, a red star on a yellow background. The nose art is a copy of an Alberto Vargas painting from his 1943 calendar.

Profile 73: P-47D-2 serial 42-8118, MSN 266, squadron number 26, *Miss Jacqueline*

This early Thunderbolt was assigned to Major David Campbell who took the 431st FS to New Guinea and led the squadron for four months until he was replaced in mid-November 1943. Note the red edge which delineates the white tail and the red line marking the rudder trim tab. The fighter, including the spiral design on the wheel hubs, is illustrated as it appeared at Durand around August 1943.

Profile 74: P-47D-2 serial 42-8082, MSN 215, squadron number 34, *Nip Nipper*

This fighter crashed in the mountains near Marilinen on 24 August 1943. The unidentified pilot baled out during a C-47 escort mission after becoming lost near the Waffar River. He walked into back into base four days later.

P-47D-2 serial 42-8118 Miss Jacqueline, as depicted in Profile 73, at Durand around August 1943.

P-47D-2 serial 42-22510 Helluva Wreck, the subject of Profile 80, as seen from a B-25D.

CHAPTER 12
342nd Fighter Squadron "The Scourgers"

The 342nd FS became the first Thunderbolt squadron to arrive in Australia, when its ground echelon disembarked at the Brisbane docks on 14 June 1943. By mid-July 1943 it had moved its headquarters to Wards 'drome, Port Moresby, from where it commenced familiarisation and C-47 escort operations to Wau, Nadzab and Marilinen alongside the other two squadrons of the 348th FG. On 13 December 1943 all three of the group's squadrons were ordered to move to Finschhafen. The 342nd FS later took up station at Saidor on 30 March 1944, then briefly Nadzab #3 before it left the main New Guinea theatre for Wakde in Dutch New Guinea on 22 May 1944. Major Raymond Gallagher took the squadron to New Guinea, before replacement by Major William Banks on 18 November 1943, who was in turn replaced by Major William Dunham on 24 May 1944.

On 18 August 1943 sixteen 342nd FS Thunderbolts came close to being destroyed by flying into mountainous terrain. Led by Captain Edward Roddy on a mission to escort C-47 transports, when they entered the Wau Valley they encountered solid overcast. Roddy led the squadron over the Upper Bubu Valley where the formation inadvertently entered cloud. No pilot was instrument rated and the formation faced the reality of mid-air collisions or flying into terrain. When they exited the cloud two Thunderbolts were missing: Lieutenant Wilfred Desilets' Thunderbolt was not located until 1996, and Lieutenant Cyril Andrews baled out. He broke his leg when he parachuted, however he was eventually returned to base with the assistance of local villagers. Roddy would concede after the war it was inexplicable that the entire squadron had not been lost.

On 5 November 1943 the deputy commander of the 342nd FS, Lieutenant Colonel Robert Rowland, led four Thunderbolts to Wewak where they fought an estimated three dozen Ki-43 *Hayabusa* and Ki-61 *Hien*. They claimed six kills from this encounter, but in fact downed two Ki-61 *Hien*. On 19 March 1944 the squadron scored one of the last aerial victories over New Guinea when arriving over Wewak at 20,000 feet they sighted sixteen Japanese fighters escorting a single a bomber well below. With an unserviceable radio, Lieutenant Robert Sutcliffe led a quartet of Thunderbolts down to attack a flight of Ki-43 *Hayabusa*, scoring a definite victory.

The 342nd FS lost a total of eighteen Thunderbolts in New Guinea, six of which were combat-related losses, including one lost to friendly fire over Cape Gloucester. The other twelve losses were due to various causes including runway collisions, mechanical failure, bad weather and landing and take-off accidents. Eight of these non-combat losses were accidents at Wards 'drome including two lost to a runway collision on 15 September 1943.

The 342nd FS logo was a diving eagle with two lightning bolts in the background, authorised in 1943.

Markings

Upon arriving in Australia, it was determined at group level that the 342nd FS would be assigned numerical identifiers in the 51 to 100 range, although two Thunderbolts used squadron numbers 101 and 102. Blue was retained as squadron colour and blue tail tips were applied a few weeks after arriving at Durand, with the squadron number applied in blue stencil on the white fin. This system was replaced around February 1944 by a blue band applied mid-tail section with the squadron number stencilled in white. This tail band system continued with the first natural metal finish P-47D-20s and P-47D-23s which started arriving in the inventory at Saidor in May 1944. In the case of these airframes the squadron number was applied in black or masked out (see Profile 82), leaving a natural metal finish stencil. Decorating wheel hubs was not as commonly applied in the 342nd FS as with the other two in the 348th FG.

P-47D-2 serial 42-8139 cruises over the foothills of the Owen Stanley Ranges to the north of Port Moresby in July 1943. The squadron number and tail tip are yet to be applied. The MSN 287 is clearly visible just forward of the national insignia.

P-47D Cindy II, which had squadron number 102, is seen here being scrapped at Nadzab in 1946.

Lieutenant Colonel Neel Kearby with the first Fiery Ginger he was assigned in New Guinea, as depicted in Profile 77.

342nd Fighter Squadron

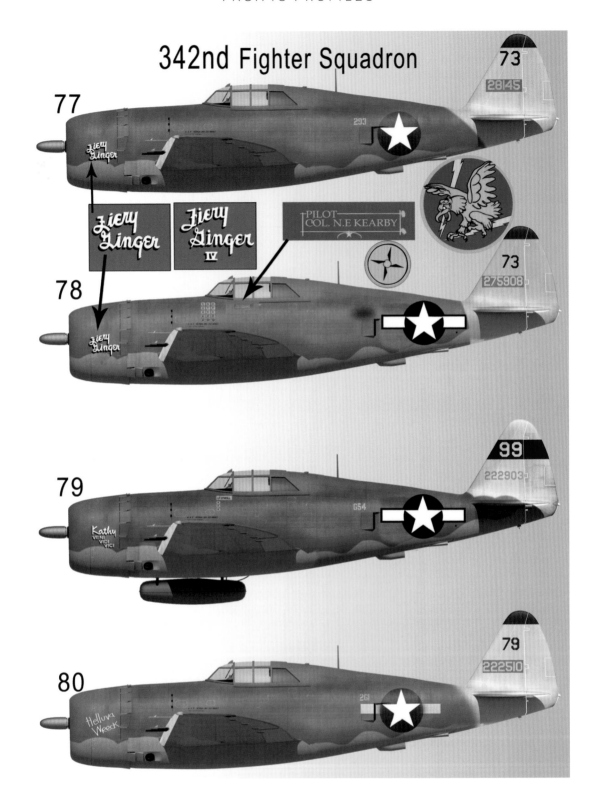

73
28145

77

Fiery Ginger

Fiery Ginger

Fiery Ginger IV

PILOT
COL. N.E KEARBY

73
275908

78

Fiery Ginger

79

Kathy
VENI
VIDI
VICI

99
222903

79
222510

80

Helluva
Wreck

Profile 77: P-47D-2 serial 42-8145, MSN 293, squadron number 73, *Fiery Ginger*

The 348th FG commander, Lieutenant Colonel Neel Kearby, was assigned three Thunderbolts while in New Guinea, not four as is often claimed (see Profile 90 for a full explanation). This fighter, P-47D-2 serial 42-8145, was lost to combat on 22 October 1943 as one of sixteen Thunderbolts escorting B-25s to Wewak. Lieutenant Ernest Ness was shot down by a Japanese fighter and baled out over Kairiru Island where he was captured and executed. The fighter is illustrated just after it had its tail tip painted blue in late July 1943 at Wards 'drome.

Profile 78: P-47D-16 serial 42-75908, MSN 4259, squadron number 73, *Fiery Ginger*

Named *Fiery Ginger* (not *Fiery Ginger III* as is often claimed), this Thunderbolt was a replacement for Kearby's first (see Profile 77). This fighter was only operated briefly by Kearby before his transfer to the 311th FS. This is confirmed by the logbook of Lieutenant Anthony Kupferer who flew his first three missions in early February 1944 from Horanda 'drome in this aircraft. Note the scoreboard of fifteen kills is further forward, just underneath the windscreen. The wheel hub was decorated in the Fifth Air Force colours of blue and yellow. The calligraphy in the name for Profiles 77 and 78 are almost identical, whereas note the "G" in Ginger for *Fiery Ginger IV* (see Profile 90) has a cursive flourish which extends downwards.

Profile 79: P-47D-11 serial 42-22903, MSN 654, squadron number 99, *Kathy Veni Vidi Vici*

This Thunderbolt was delivered to the 342nd FS in December 1943 and was assigned to Lieutenant Lawrence O'Neill.

Profile 80: P-47D-2 serial 42-22510, MSN 261, squadron number 79, *Helluva Wreck*

One of the last D-2s to be produced, the fighter had a field-modified star and bar. The crew assignments are unknown; however, it has no record of accidental or combat damage.

The line-up at Nadzab #3 in early October 1943 This was the last known photo taken of Kearby's Fiery Ginger (Profile 77), with the Thunderbolt visible just behind the RAAF Vengeance.

342nd Fighter Squadron

Profile 81: P-47D-2 serial 42-8152, MSN 300, squadron number 51, *Cabby*

Assigned to Lieutenant Raymond Gallagher, on 18 February 1944 Lieutenant David Riley collided with another aircraft shortly after departing Finschhafen and baled out. *Cabby* fell into the sea however Riley was rescued. Back in the US, Gallagher had named his P-47C *City of Hartford*.

Profile 82: P-47D-21 serial 42-26492, MSN 2069, squadron number 83

This was one of the first natural metal finish Thunderbolts to be delivered to the 342nd FS and was flown to Saidor in late April 1944 where it is illustrated as a brand-new aircraft. After the squadron moved from the theatre, it painted the rudders of all its Thunderbolts in the pre-war red, white and blue striped marking.

Profile 83: P-47D-4 serial 42-22694, MSN 445, squadron number 64, *Sylvia / Racine Belle*

When he was assigned this Thunderbolt in November 1943, Lieutenant Marvin Grant named it *Sylvia*. His crew chief named it *Racine Belle* after his hometown of Racine in Wisconsin on the cowl on the other side. The fighter left the factory with red-outlined national insignia, however, it is unclear whether these were painted out in the field.

Profile 84: P-47D-23 serial 42-27886, MSN 1548, squadron number 84, *Sylvia / Racine Belle*

In late May 1944 (promoted to captain) Marvin Grant received this natural metal finish Thunderbolt as a replacement for Profile 83. His crew chief decided to keep the cowl of the original Olive Drab P-47D-4 which they attached to the new fighter. Grant painted the white stripe with red piping down the side of the fuselage so the fighter could more readily be identified as a flight leader. The fighter was later transferred to the 40th FS where it is illustrated in Profile 26.

Squadron number 101 during a visit to Durand 'drome in late 1943. This was one of two 342nd FS squadron numbers allocated outside of the regular 51 to 100 range.

342nd Fighter Squadron

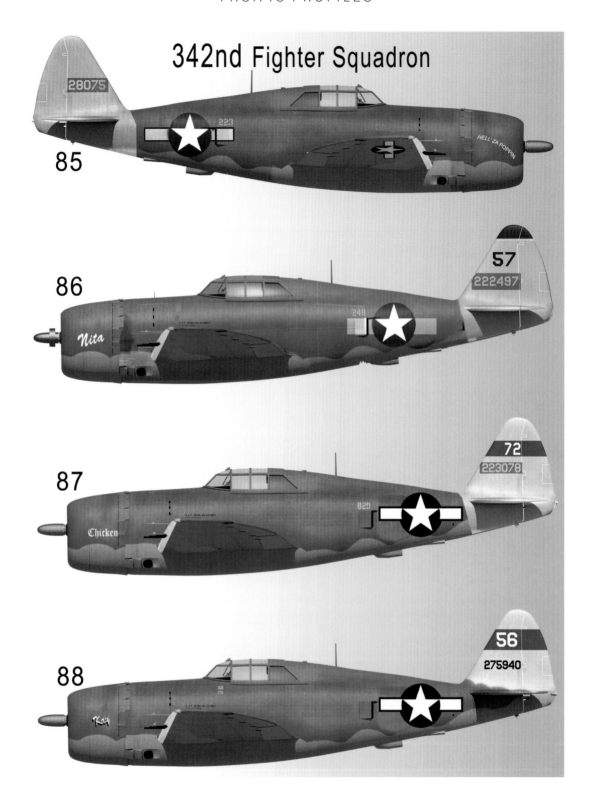

28075

223

HELL'ZA POPPIN

85

57
222497

248

Nita

86

72
223078

829

Chicken

87

56
275940

Kay

88

Profile 85: P-47D-2 serial 42-8075, MSN 223, *Hell'za poppin*

This Thunderbolt is illustrated when it first appeared at Seven-Mile 'drome just after its July 1943 delivery flight, and without a blue fin tip or squadron number. It was damaged on 14 September 1943 during take-off from this airfield and was repaired, however it was struck off following a landing accident, again at Seven-Mile, on 22 October 1943. Note that white bars with blue borders were added early in its career.

Profile 86: P-47D-2 serial 42-22497, MSN 248, squadron number 57, *Nita*

This fighter was lost on 22 October 1943 when the 342nd FS alongside the 341st FS were assigned to escort B-25s to Wewak. Three of the P-47s including that flown by Lieutenant Wynans Frankfort ran low on fuel on the return journey after becoming lost over the expansive Fly River delta. Frankfort baled out low at around a thousand feet, breaking a rib as did so. He followed the river and found a village with friendly locals took him to a plantation house from where he was returned to his unit by PBY. The fighter is illustrated on the day it was lost, with added white bars to the national insignia. It is unclear who named the fighter.

Profile 87: P-47D-11 serial 42-23078, MSN 829, squadron number 72, *Chicken*

Delivered to the 342nd FS in early February 1944, this fighter was assembled at the Commonwealth Aircraft Corporation factory near Melbourne. The squadron number was applied across the revised blue band marking introduced around this time.

Profile 88: P-47D-16 serial 42-75940, MSN 4291, squadron number 56, *Kay*

This Thunderbolt was assigned to Lieutenant Wynans Frankfort at the end of February 1944 who had already survived a bale out from Profile 86. The blue tail band with squadron number 56 is indicative of the new markings system introduced around February 1944. Frankfort was lost in this fighter when attacking Biak on 27 May 1944.

Kearby in the cockpit of P-47D-16 42-75908, as shown in Profile 78, at Wards 'drome in November 1943. A slightly later photo shows a total of fifteen victory flags (see page 98).

A close examination of the Fiery Ginger IV display at the National Museum of the US Air Force. Whilst it is debateable whether the red lines surrounding the national insignia were painted over in the field, it is regrettable that this field-modified national insignia is wrong. The restorers have added white bars to a single circular star. However, as with all D-4s, Fiery Ginger IV left the factory with relevant Army/Navy (AN) Markings Specification AN-1-9A dated 28 June 1943, with the first red-bordered insignia applied in Republic's factory in July 1943 (see Profile 90).

Neel Kearby with P-47D-16 serial 42-75908 Fiery Ginger, as depicted in Profile 78. His fifteenth claim was made on 3 December 1943 which dates this photo a few days subsequent. Note the victory flags are applied more forward than those on his subsequent Fiery Ginger IV which he flew with Fifth Fighter Command (see Profile 90).

CHAPTER 13
Fifth Fighter Command Headquarters

In September 1942, Major General George Kenney structured the USAAF Fifth Air Force into three commands presided over by his deputy Brigadier General Ennis Whitehead. Fifth Service Command was briefly under the command of Major General Rush Lincoln before passing to Major Victor Bertrandis. This was based at Garbutt, Townsville, where Fifth Bomber Command under Brigadier General Kenneth Walker was similarly based. Fifth Fighter Command was led by Colonel Paul "Squeeze" Wurtsmith from 11 November 1942. By early 1944 Fifth Fighter Command Headquarters had moved to Nadzab.

Fifth Fighter Command Headquarters was primarily an operational and administrative umbrella for Fifth Air Force fighter operations, however it also had an operational detachment to which top-scoring pilots were posted. These sometimes flew on a "roving commission" basis where required. On 12 November 1943 Lieutenant Colonel Neel Kearby was transferred to Fifth Fighter Command, transferring leadership of the 348th FG to Lieutenant Colonel Robert Rowland. Despite being nominally assigned administrative duties, Kearby still flew combat missions. Command Headquarters fighters were serviced by the host units from which they were borrowed, and accordingly also carried the markings of their host units.

On display at the National Museum of the US Air Force is a restored P-47D painted as Neel Kearby's Fiery Ginger IV. The fin of the original aircraft is on display adjacent.

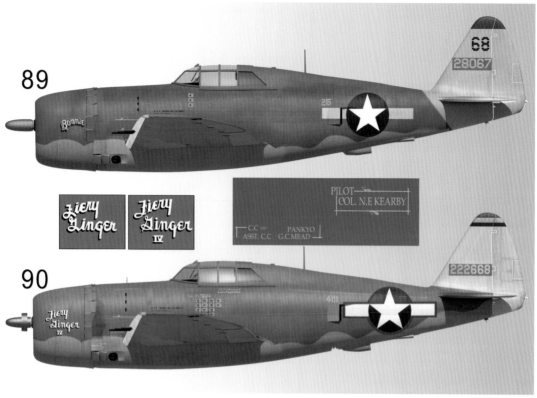

89

90

PILOT
COL. N.E KEARBY

C.C
ASST. C.C

PANKYO
G.C.MEAD

Neel Kearby looks at Staff Sergeant Pankyo (with back to camera), a crew chief he employed from the 341st FS to maintain his fighter. This shot was taken at Wards 'drome very soon after Kearby took delivery of Fiery Ginger IV.

Profile 89: P-47D-2 serial 42-8067, MSN 215, squadron number 68, *Bonnie*

Captain William "Dinghy" Dunham became the second leading Thunderbolt ace in the Pacific after Colonel Neel Kearby. Dunham flew this Thunderbolt to Wards 'drome in July 1943 with the 342nd FS. By end of December 1943 *Bonnie* had seven Japanese flags on the airframe. These were for victories which included: 11 October (one Ki-43 *Hayabusa*), 16 October (two Ki-43 *Hayabusa*), 19 October (an F1M2 Pete floatplane near Kairiru Island) and one Ki-43 *Hayabusa* on 22 December. After taking home leave, Dunham returned to combat in November 1944, was promoted to major and appointed commander of the newly created 460th FS before subsequently becoming the 348th FG operations officer. When he was promoted to lieutenant colonel in August 1945 he became the group's deputy commander. The fighter is illustrated as it appeared a few days after Dunham's two claims of 16 October 1943, giving a total of three flags. Although assigned to the 342nd FS, Dunham flew with Kearby on several Fifth Fighter Command missions.

Profile 90: P-47D-4 serial 42-22668, MSN 419, *Fiery Ginger IV*

The location, markings and identity of this Thunderbolt have been consistently misrepresented over the years. Colonel Neel Kearby was shot down in his fighter, his third and last assigned to him in the theatre, on 5 March 1944 behind Dagua airfield. The loss occurred when five 77th *Sentai* Ki-43-II *Hayabusa* launched from Dagua to protect some Ki-48 bombers that had been attacked by P-47s in the circuit area. Kearby turned a full circle at low altitude, likely to ascertain the fate of the bombers. As he completed his circle a *Hayabusa* loomed into view on a beam attack. Dunham banked towards the perpetrator and opened fire, reporting that it crashed in flames. Kearby suddenly changed course to head into the arc of Dunham's protective gunfire, however it appears Kearby was hit by bullets before Dunham's return fire could deter his attacker. Warrant Officer Mitoma Koichi and Sergeant Aoyagi Hiroshi claimed a Thunderbolt each. Aoyagi was a rookie pilot who had just arrived in the theatre with barely 200 hours flying time. Kearby managed to bale out of the fighter just before it went down, and his remains were recovered in 1946. The markings have since been confirmed from the wreckage, parts of which remained intact.

On the tip of the fin this fighter has the colours of red, yellow and blue, the three colours of each 348th FG squadron. The fighter was a P-47D-4 which left the factory with an outlined red star and bar —not a modified single star with white bars added, as incorrectly portrayed by the USAF Museum. Both Profile 1 and this fighter came from the same batch of P-47D-4s, and the post-war wreckage from both sites indicate both left the factory with red outlined insignia on both fuselage and wings. Perhaps they were painted over in the field, however numerous photos of *Fiery Ginger IV* show the red outline still extant towards the end of its career. The fighter is illustrated around Christmas 1943 showing 17 victories, the 17th being a Ki-61 over Dagua on 23 December 1943, just after Kearby took delivery of it.

It is useful to outline the mistaken assumptions made over the years, leading to the wrong conclusion that Kearby had four assigned Thunderbolts in New Guinea, instead of three. The deduction has been made as his last Thunderbolt was named *Fiery Ginger IV*, however the fact is his first and second Thunderbolts were not named I and II, just having the name *Fiery Ginger*. Note the slightly different "G" in *Fiery Ginger* between Profiles 78 and 90.

The timeline of Kearby's three Thunderbolts are:

1. His first (Profile 77) was lost to combat with another pilot on 22 October 1943.

2. The second was a P-47D-16 (as per Profile 78). This airframe was transferred via a service squadron to the 311th FS in early January 1944. The logbook of 311th FS pilot Lieutenant Anthony Kupferer records his first three missions in early February 1944 from Horanda 'drome in this aircraft. Kearby was photographed (see page 98) with this Thunderbolt with fifteen victories, meaning the photo was taken after his fifteenth victory of 3 December 1943.

3. The third was *Fiery Ginger IV* which he received in the period between 4 and 23 December 1943. A photo of Kearby sitting in *Fiery Ginger IV* shows 17 victory flags (the 16th and 17th claims occurred on 22 and 23 December 1943).

So why did Kearby name his third Thunderbolt "IV"? Possibly, he named the P-47C Thunderbolt he trained on in the US as *Fiery Ginger*, making it the first in a series of four. Regardless, the service records indicate clearly that Kearby was only assigned three Thunderbolts while serving in New Guinea.

This is the last known photo taken of Fiery Ginger IV with 22 kill flags.

CHAPTER 14
Combat Replacement Training Center

After the Fifth and Thirteenth Air Forces advanced to the Netherlands East Indies and then the Philippines, Nadzab continued to serve as a staging base where the Combat Replacement Training Center (CRTC) was established. The unit was part of the 360th Service Group, with engineering support from the 8th Service Group. The first CRTC commander was Colonel John Henebry, who had previously served as commander of the 3rd Bombardment Group. The concept behind the unit was to give incoming crews assigned to both air forces combat training and experience before they were assigned to frontline units.

The unit operated a varied inventory including the A-20G, B-25 Mitchell, B-24 Liberator, P-47D Thunderbolt and finally the P-51D Mustang. In addition, there were an assortment of liaison aircraft including C-45s and L-5s, and instrument trainers in the form of the BT-13B Valiant. The 1st Composite Fighter Unit was created within the CRTC; however, its operations remain almost forgotten. CRTC crews flew combat missions over bypassed targets including Wewak and even Rabaul until 30 June 1945, after which the unit was ordered to advance to Clark Field in the Philippines. Some missions supported the Australian Army in its 1945 "mopping up" campaigns along New Guinea's northern coast. At the end of the war the unit's remaining aircraft were abandoned at Nadzab and later scrapped.

The tail of P-47D-11 serial 43-25481, the subject of Profile 92, in the New Guinea jungle shortly after it was identified in 1985.

Combat Replacement Training Center

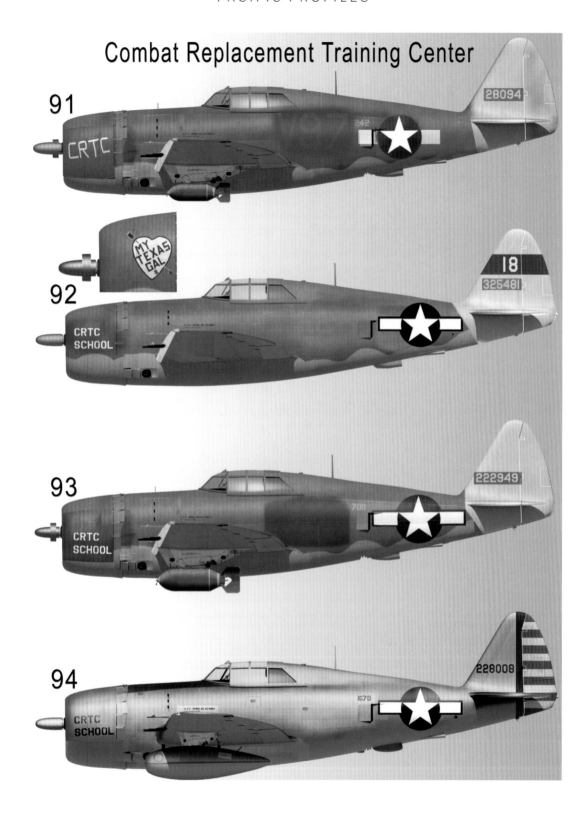

91

92

93

94

Profile 91: P-47D-2 serial 42-8094, MSN 242

This fighter previously served with the 311th FS as *Louisville Lady* (see Profile 51). The nose art was painted over and replaced by hand painted CRTC lettering, however the original tail markings were left extant.

Profile 92: P-47D-11 serial 43-25481, MSN 1058

This fighter was first assigned to Captain Andrew Lytle of the 340th FS who named it *My Texas Gal II*. When it was replaced by a natural metal finish Thunderbolt (see Profile 61), it was transferred to CRTC, as illustrated here. The nose art was painted over and replaced by the CRTC stencil; however, the original tail markings were left extant. The fighter went missing mid-afternoon on 30 April 1945 when flown by Lieutenant Allen Hermann after departing Nadzab #1 for a local training flight. The wreckage of the aircraft was identified in May 1985 in the hills behind Marilinen.

Profile 93: P-47D-11 serial 42-22949, MSN 700

This aircraft was transferred into the CRTC from the 311th FS, and retained that unit's blue cowl panel. It departed Nadzab Strip #1 on 12 May 1945 when flown by Lieutenant Harold Wurtz who had agreed to take a Red Cross nurse, Miss Harriet Gowen, for a mid-afternoon joyflight. The aircraft was not seen again after departure, and in fact crashed fourteen miles west of Nadzab. It drove into soft earth at high speed almost vertically, the engine burying itself a good four metres into the earth. The crash site was was discovered in 1996 and identified the following year.

Profile 94: P-47D-23 serial 42-28008, MSN 1670

Once later model "bubbletops" started appearing in the Philippines inventory earlier "razorback" P-47Ds including natural metal finish ones were sent to operate with the CRTC. This one crashed at Nadzab #1 on 28 April 1945 during a take-off accident and was destroyed, however the pilot survived.

The end of an era. Captain Bill Dunham (third from left) with his new natural metal finish P-47D-23 serial 42-27884. Named Bonnie, it was received in early June 1944 and was decorated with nine kill markings. The other pilots (left to right) are Lieutenants Edward Wyroba, Edward Wood and Franklin Love, all standing behind a scoreboard with the emblem of the 342nd FS. Dunham will soon leave that unit to take command of the 460th FS.

SOURCES & ACKNOWLEDGMENTS

Research for this volume draws exclusively on primary sources. The author's extensive collection of photos and notes from field trips contains a labyrinth of information drawn from many years. It is impractical to list this minutiae, other than to cite the mainstream sources below.

Known Wreck list, Port Moresby Control Tower, 1960s

Headquarters Fifth Air Force Special Orders No. 272, 29 September 1943

Website www.pacificwrecks.com

Allied Translator and Interpreter Section (ATIS) Reports

Allied Air Force Intelligence Summaries (AWM)

ANGAU patrol officer reports of Allied crash sites 1940s-1970s

Republic Aircraft Corporation (Engineering and relevant records)

P-47 markings details from relevant Individual Deceased Personnel Files (IDPF)

Field Trips by author throughout New Guinea and the Pacific, 1964-2017

Pacific Aircraft Historical Society - Wreck Data Sheets

PNG Colonial Office - Civil Administration Records

PNG Museum of Modern History, files and records

Aircraft Movement Entries, Townsville Control Tower, 1943-45

Field notes of Robert Greinart and John Douglas, wreck sites, PNG, 2011-2019

Microfilms/ official records

Fifth AF Units (via Maxwell AFB), including unit and maintenance and repair sheets: 5th Air Force Establishment, Fifth Fighter Command, Combat Replacement Training Center (CRTC), 8th FG, 348th, 49th , 58th, 35th FG, and 360th Service Group; 9th, 36th, 39th, 40th, 41st, 69th, 310th, 311th, 340th, 341st and 342nd FS, Fifth Fighter Command, 14th Tow Target Squadron, 1947th Aviation Utilities Company, 5297th Chemical Training Company (attached to CRTC), 8th SG, 1794th Ordinance Aviation, 1811th Ordinance Aviation, 47th Service Squadron (SS), 455th SS, 370th SS, 7th Airdrome Squadron (AS), 301st AS, 868th Engineer Aviation Battalion (attached to CRTC at Nadzab).

Index of Names

Ahern, Lieutenant John 59

Alber, Lieutenant George 25

Andress Lieutenant Crystal 61

Andrews, Lieutenant Cyril 89

Aoyagi Hiroshi, Sergeant 9, 101

Arthur, Lieutenant Wilbert 25

Atkinson, Lieutenant Colonel Gwen 49, 55, 63

Banks, Major William 89

Bertrandis, Major Victor 99

Blair, Captain Sam 9, 83

Bohman, Captain Carl 47

Bong, Major Richard Ira 33

Booty, Captain Donald 55

Bridgers, Staff Sergeant Ben 65

Brown, Lieutenant Jack 67

Bullington, Major Thomas 9, 63, 64

Campbell, Major David 79, 87

Capp, Al 37

Carpenter, Major Hervey 71

Carter, Major Landis 63

Carter, Captain Otto 13

Carter, Lieutenant William 73

Chadwell, Lieutenant Leroy 59

Cooper, Gary 39

Cracey, Captain Charles 55

Davis, Lieutenant Thomas 37

Della, Lieutenants George 83

Denton, Major Harris 33

Desilets, Lieutenant Wilfred 89

Dikovitsky, Lieutenant Michael "Mike" 75

Donar, Lieutenant Francis 49

Dorko, Staff Sergeant A 83

Dunham, Major William 9, 89, 101, 106

Evans, Lieutenant Ray 67

Fallier, Lieutenant Nick 35

Fish, Lieutenant Donald 51

Frankfort, Lieutenant Wynans 97

Frintner, Lieutenant Henry 47

Frost, Lieutenant John 32

Galik, Lieutenant Samuel 79

Gallagher, Major Raymond 89, 95

Gerrity, Lieutenant John 39

Giroux, Lieutenant Gordon 29

Gowan, Miss Harriet 9, 105

Graham, Lieutenant William 9, 63, 64

Grant, Captain Marvin 95

Grosshuesch, Lieutenant Leroy 37

Gustavson, Lieutenant Robert 47

Haislip, Lieutenant James 25

Harding, Lieutenant Wallace 73

Harris, Lieutenant James 23, 26

Hartsfield, Lieutenant John 45

Heckerman, Lieutenant Arthur 29

Henebry, Colonel John 103

Herbert, Captain James 39

Hermann, Lieutenant Allen 105

Hnatio, Lieutenant Myron 75

Hoyt, Lieutenant Edward 45

Huyck, Staff Sergeant Frank 59

Jander, Captain Don 63, 65

Jeannes, Lieutenant Raby 47

Johnson, Major Gerald 21-23, 25

Johnson, Lieutenant Guy 53

Jordan, Major Wallace 21, 23

Karavedas, Lieutenant Spiros 61

Kearby, Colonel Neel 7, 9, 71, 79, 91, 93, 97-102

Kenney, Major General George 99

Kitternick 59

Klemovich, Major Thomas 63

Koga Keiji, Lieutenant 71

Koyama Shigeru, Captain 79

Kupferer, Lieutenant Anthony 64, 67, 93

Kyro, Lieutenant Erick 45

Leatherwood 59

Lincoln, Major General Rush 99

Lindberg, Charles 8, 33

Lolos, Lieutenant John 78, 81, 83, 87

Love, Lieutenant Franklin 106

Lutes, Lieutenant Marion 23

Lytle, Captain Andrew 75

Marston, Lieutenant Art 65

Masuzawa Masanao, Lieutenant 49

Matsumoto Kunio, Major 9

McCleldon, Lieutenant Adrian 7

McClure, Major Jack Jr 55, 59

McDonald, Captain Charles 71

McMullen, Captain Harry 53

Milner, Lieutenant Edward 9

Mitoma Koichi, Warrant Officer 9, 101

Moore, Major John 79, 80, 85

Muraoka Shinichi, Major 8

Namai Kiyoshi, Captain 9, 63, 64

Nelson, Captain 47

Ness, Lieutenant Ernest 93

Noble, Flying Officer Denby 43

O'Leary, Lieutenant James 64, 67

O'Neill, Lieutenant Lawrence 93

Oglesby, Lieutenant Howard 26

Okuma Kaoru, Lieutenant Commander 35

Oldren, Captain Harry "Oddie" 63

Pankyo, Staff Sergeant 100

Park, Lieutenant Edwards 43, 47

Perkins, Lieutenant 30

Powell, Lieutenant Robert 62, 65

Querns, Lieutenant Jim 37

Riley, Lieutenant David 95

Ritter, Lieutenant William 67

Roddy, Captain Edward 89

Rogers, Lieutenant William 35

Rohrken, Sergeant Erich 67

Rothman, Lieutenant Marvin 63

Rowland, Lieutenant Colonel Robert 81, 85, 89, 99

Sakata Koichi, Lieutenant 79

Schrik, Lieutenant John 8

Self, Major Milton 49, 51

Shimanto Kikuo, Sergeant 79

Sutcliffe, Lieutenant Robert 89

Sutherland, Staff Sergeant Robert 61

Suzuki Sozaku, Sergeant Major 79

Teranishi Tamiya, Lieutenant Colonel 79

Theed, Lieutenant Clement Jr 59

Thomas, Lieutenant Philip 41

Thorpe, Lieutenant Robert 35

Toda Shiro, Sergeant 79

Tuman, Captain Howard 49

Vargas, Alberto 53, 73, 87

Walker, Brigadier General Kenneth 99

Wandrey, Lieutenant Ralph 25

Weeks, Captain Arthur 83

Weidmeyer, Lieutenant Raymond 47, 48

Whitehead, Brigadier General Ennis 99

Wiecks, Captain Max 71

Wolf, Captain Lester 55

Wood, Lieutenant Edward 106

Wood, Lieutenant George 49

Wooley, Captain Carey 47

Wurtsmith, Colonel Paul "Squeeze" 99

Wurtz, Lieutenant Harold 9, 105

Wyroba, Lieutenant Edward 106

Young, Chic 45

Young, Captain John 39